WHEN
CHRISTIANS
ROAMED
THE EARTH

Is the Bible-Believing Church

Headed for Extinction?

DATE DUE	
JUN 0 3 2003	
11/16/03	
APR 2 7 2005	

THE LIBRARY STORE #47-0130

WHEN CHRISTIANS ROAMED THE EARTH

Is the Bible-Believing Church
Headed for Extinction?

HENRY M. MORRIS • KEN HAM
JACK CUOZZO • JOHN D. MORRIS
CARL WIELAND • JONATHAN HENRY

Master
Books

First printing: December 2001

Copyright © 2002 by Master Books, Inc. All rights reserved. No part of this book may be used or reproduced in any manner whatsoever without written permission of the publisher, except in the case of brief quotations in articles and reviews. For information write: Master Books, Inc., P.O. Box 727, Green Forest, AR 72638.

ISBN: 0-89051-319-8
Library of Congress Catalog Number: 99-67334

Printed in the United States of America

Please visit our website for other great titles:
www.masterbooks.net

For information regarding author interviews, contact
the publicity department at (870) 438-5288.

Contents

Preface

In 2001, explorer Robert Ballard, who discovered the wreck of the *Titanic* in 1985, began an intriguing search of the Black Sea. He wanted to find evidence of Noah's flood.

Geology studies had indicated that a massive flood had taken place at the site sometime in the last several thousand years. Ballard's team did in fact find evidence of human civilization on ancient shorelines underneath the Black Sea.

Interestingly, though, the expedition wasn't about proving Noah's flood. Rather, it was launched to find the source of the Genesis "myth." After all, reasoned researchers, the event as recorded in the Bible couldn't be historically true. Indeed, media all over the world touted the discoveries, always linking them as sources of various flood myths found in many countries and cultures, particularly the Babylonian *Enuma Elish*, which detailed the heroic tale of Gilgamesh, who endured the flood.

This is where we've come to in the Christian West. Far from our roots as Bible-believing men and women, we are now on the slippery slope of unbelief. Generations of people have seen their own faith shipwrecked by the spurious theories of scholars who have systematically attacked the Bible. Men like Thomas Huxley, Herbert Spencer, and Harry Emerson Fosdick followed the lead of the German Higher Critics, who worked to present the Old Testament as the evolving spiritual myth of the Hebrews. This, of course, stands in stark contrast to the Bible as the majestic word of God.

So we have these two very different world views: Scripture is revelation from God/Scripture is man's first attempts at shaping a primitive theology. The implications are huge.

To counter the big lie that Genesis was influenced by Mesopotamian myth, several leading creationist authors and speakers have been brought together to present clear evidence that the Bible is exactly what it claims to be, and that its cosmogonies are the true account of the origin of all things.

You will enjoy reading about startling, firsthand research on human origins by people like John Morris and Jack Cuozzo. You will no doubt be fascinated by the subject of the search for extraterrestrial life by Jonathan Henry. Ken Ham and Carl Wieland look at the implications of evolutionary thought on the Church, while Henry Morris traces what he has so aptly called the Long War Against God.

This book raises profound questions, first for the Church.

Once, Christians who boldly taught from Scripture were in abundance. They spread the Good News far and wide, preaching the whole gospel. Sadly, as the subtle-yet-lethal message of uniformitarianism gained wide acceptance, more and more people turned away from the life-affirming Bible, believing instead that it is a mistake-ridden, inaccurate collection of outdated religion.

Today, we see the cheapening and chipping away of

our Christian heritage, as even many prominent ministries subscribe to evolutionary-based theories of origins. Sweeping under the rug the critical issue of creation vs. evolution, it is felt by many that such discussions are divisive and hurtful. On this we can agree: these issues are divisive, for they draw a clear line between faith in the God of the Bible and a god who used a brutal system of trial-and-error "creation." Hurtful because it requires people everywhere to take a hard look at what they believe and why. When someone asks us why the Resurrection could possibly be historically true, if we compromise on the historicity of Genesis . . . how do we answer?

This question joins with many others (the Virgin Birth, the Cross, Jesus' miracles, the Second Coming) as people the world over are desperate to believe in something saving.

Our opportunity to present the life-changing message of Christ's love pivots on the all-important veracity of Genesis.

Will true Christianity survive and thrive in the uncertain days ahead? Or will it become extinct, like the giant reptiles that grace our museums today, used as propaganda by those committed to atheistic naturalism?

Now is the time for Christians to recognize the remarkable claims of the Bible. For a frightened world, our presentation of the gospel means the difference between life and death. Even Christ himself looked at the future and said:

> When the Son of Man comes, will He really find faith on the earth? (Luke 18:8).

How will He find you?

Chapter 1

THE CONFLICT OF THE AGES

Henry M. Morris

We are living today in what many are calling a post-modern age — an age when there are no absolutes and almost anything goes. A more realistic designation, however, might be the Post-Christian Age, when almost any kind of belief and practice except biblical Christianity is tolerated and even encouraged.

Our nation was founded on biblical principles, as a Christian nation, largely by founding fathers who were serious about their faith in God and the Bible. This faith was implicit, not only in the writings of the pilgrims and other early settlers, but also later in the Declaration of Independence and then the Constitution with its Bill of Rights. The various state constitutions and court decisions (at least those prior to the 20th century) reflected the same Judeo-Christian faith of the fathers. Our laws had been largely derived from the British common law, which in turn had been mainly developed from biblical principles — both the Mosaic laws and the teachings of Christ.[1] The early schools and colleges of our country likewise had built their programs around the same foundation, freely including the Bible and prayer in their studies and activities.

But now a great apostasy has set in. Although it began with the rise of deism in the 18th century, the real roots of the apostasy are in the resurgence of ancient evolutionism in the form of Darwinism during the late 19th and early 20th centuries. This system had soon triumphed in the schools and courts (under the guise of separating church and state and science from religion). These developments eventually fomented the infamous student revolution in the sixties, with its accompanying emphases on anti-nationalism, sexual freedom, one-worldism, and anti-Christianity in general.

These bad seeds and bitter roots have come to full flower in this post-Christian age. Ancient pagan religions are experiencing a great revival in the form of a plethora of New-Age cults, accompanied by tremendous expansion of eastern ethnic religions (Hinduism, Buddhism, etc.) and militant Islam, even here in "Christian" America — even more so in the nominally Christian (or more realistically post-Christian) nations of Europe, South America, and Australia.

The moral standards of much of the world are rapidly "slouching toward Gomorrah" as Judge Robert Bork has expressed it. Even in the United States, its twice-elected immoral president Bill Clinton not only was a notorious philanderer and adulterer, but also had been a persistent liar and even perjurer (with impeachment swirling all around him). Even worse was the fact that his political party and (seemingly) 75 percent of the population seemed to approve of him.

Some may argue that the American people are still quite "religious." About 90 percent will say they believe in God (but their concept of God is often radically different in nature from the God of the Bible), and about 50 percent will say they have been "born again," (but they often are thinking in terms of some religious experience drastically different from biblical regeneration through personal repentance and faith in Jesus Christ, as described in the Holy Scriptures (John 3:3–8; Rom. 6:1–14; Titus 3:5–7; 1 Pet. 1:23; etc.).

The "mainline" churches, seminaries, and denominational colleges have largely capitulated to theological liberalism and often to New Age concepts. The same is true to a lesser degree among a significant number of evangelical churches and educational institutions.

There are, of course, a goodly number of American evangelical and fundamentalist churches and schools that still believe in biblical inerrancy and the saving gospel of Christ, and I believe that God has withheld divine judgment on America thus far mainly because of this remnant of genuine Christian believers in the nation.

But even here there is cause for concern. There is much less emphasis on systematic study of the Bible and solid Christian literature than there was a generation ago, with more emphasis on psychological counseling and social involvement. Adultery, pre-marital sex, divorce, and other evils are much more common among Bible-believing Christians than they used to be.

Most Christian bookstores carry few solid and substantive Christian books nowadays, catering more to frothy devotional and self-help books, and also to so-called "holy hardware" and other such items as found in secular gift stores. The seemingly endless parade of new Bible translations, promoted to replace the beautiful God-honoring, time-tested King James Bible, has caused great confusion and a significant decrease in genuine Bible knowledge. Contemporary repetitive "worship choruses" have largely displaced the beautiful Christian hymns and meaningful gospel songs that Christians used to sing, and this is true even in most Bible-believing churches. Emotionalism has replaced thoughtful reverence and insightful Bible exposition in too many church services and evangelistic crusades. I have been actively involved in such churches all my 80+ years and personally feel a great sense of spiritual loss because of these sad trends.

We need to consider seriously the poignant question of the Lord Jesus Christ. "When the Son of Man cometh, shall He find (the) faith on the earth?" (Luke 18:8; KJV). As we get deeper into the last days, and opposition to true Christianity intensifies (remember 2 Tim. 3:1, 12, 13), will our present faith and practice stand the test? In this country, we Christians have enjoyed almost four hundred years of religious freedom and even politico-legal favor, but this situation is rapidly deteriorating. The enemies of biblical Christianity are becoming stronger all the time and would like, if they can, to totally eliminate true biblical faith from the earth.

But actually, this is nothing really new. God's people have lived under the threat of violent opposition ever since Cain killed his brother, Abel. The whole world population, except for Noah's family, was destroyed by the God-sent flood because of their wickedness, and then God later had to disperse the peoples at Babel because of their new rebellion against Him. His remnant of chosen people were later enslaved by the Egyptians and, after they became a free nation, under Moses, the later prophets and other God-fearing Israelites "had trial of cruel mockings and scourgings, yea, moreover of bonds and imprisonment" by their own leaders (Heb. 11:36). Finally, Christ was crucified by both Jews and Gentiles, and then His followers likewise were persecuted. In fact, He told them that "the time cometh, that whosoever killeth you will think that He doeth God service" (John 16:2). And so it has been, all through history. Bible-believing Christians have been persecuted successively by the Romans, the Moslems, and even by other professing Christians.

In this country, and other Christian countries after the Reformation, thankfully, the widespread circulation of the Bible and the modern missionary movement has been accompanied by a long period of freedom from all but isolated incidents of persecution. But this period is soon coming to a close.

In this past century, there were mass persecutions of Christians in Russia, China, and other communist countries, as well as Nazi Germany (along with the Jewish holocaust). More recently have come the persecutions in Nigeria, Sudan, Rwanda, and other "liberated" African countries, not to mention political actions — even in America — against Bible teaching, prayer, and Christian witnessing in schools and other government institutions. Especially onerous and harmful in its long-range effects has been the promotion of evolutionism and anti-creationism in the schools. Many of the bitter fruits of such indoctrination will be discussed in more detail in other chapters of this book.

Right now, however, we need to recognize that all this is part of Satan's long war against God. It has been going on for ages, and will continue until Christ returns and banishes Satan and all his allies, both human and demonic, from the earth.

The Two Views of the World and Life

Indeed, a cosmic warfare has been raging between God and the devil ever since the beginning. Every age, every nation has been involved. Each of us is also involved on one side or the other and this becomes apparent in our respective views of the world and its meaning.

There are really only two basic world views. Either we can seek to explain the origin, development, and meaning of all things in terms of continuing natural processes or we cannot. One world view is expressed in terms of evolution and the other one by divine creation. These two perspectives embrace everything in the world of sense, knowledge, and understanding. We must believe in either one world view or the other; we cannot really believe both because each is the opposite of the other. One is God-centered; the other is creature-centered. Creator or creature. Creation versus evolution.

This conflict has been going on since the very beginning in one form or another. When we evaluate these two world views scientifically, we find that all of the genuine scientific evidence supports creation and that not a single real fact of science supports evolution. We shall look at some of that evidence in subsequent chapters.

But there is also another very effective way to evaluate this conflict, a way that the Lord Jesus himself gave us. He said, "Ye shall know them by their fruits. . . . A good tree cannot bring forth evil fruit, neither can a corrupt tree bring forth good fruit" (Matt. 7:16–18).We can evaluate these two world views not only in terms of the scientific evidence, but also in terms of the fruit which they have produced. When we do this, it soon becomes evident that the creationist world view, the creationist tree, has borne good fruits whereas the evolutionist tree has produced only evil fruits. That will be the main theme of this book.

The creationist world view has produced sound doctrine, good systems, and good practices. The evolutionist tree, on the other hand, universally has produced bad doctrine, bad fruits, and bad practices. That may sound extreme, but I believe that it can be documented compellingly in ways even most Christian people are not aware of.

First, in support of the thesis that the basic conflict between world views is one involving evolution versus special creation, or Satan versus God, let me mention a few verses of Scripture. The Lord Jesus Christ said himself in John 8:44 that the devil is the father of liars. He is a liar; he is the great deceiver. Revelation 12:9 reveals that Satan is the one who has deceived the whole world. In 2 Corinthians 4:4 we read: "If our gospel be hid, it is hid to them that are lost: In whom the god of this world [that is, the devil] hath blinded the minds of them which believe not, lest the light of the glorious gospel of Christ, who is the image of God, should shine unto them." If people cannot understand the gospel, it is because their minds have been blinded by the devil. He is the great deceiver. He appears sometimes as an angel of light and he has so-called ministers of righteousness, but he is basically *the* deceiver. And as 1 John 5:19 says, "The whole world lies in [the wicked one]." Evolution is, in fact, Satan's great lie, with which he seeks to persuade men and women to abandon faith in their Creator.

One great example of the creationist tree producing good fruit is the fact that our own nation was founded upon creationism! Our American nation, with all of its tradition of religious liberty and freedom, was founded upon the premise of creation! The Declaration of Independence asserts that we have been endowed by our Creator with certain unalienable rights. Creationism is also implicit in the Constitution and in the writings of the founding fathers. Even men like Thomas Jefferson and Ben Franklin, who may not have been what we would call fundamental, Bible-believing Christians, at least believed in supernatural creation. Thomas Jefferson explicitly rejected the idea of evolution in his writings. Ben Franklin also said that he believed in a Creator who had created the world. So did George Washington, James Madison, Alexander Hamilton, and even Tom Paine. The founding fathers of our nation were practically all creationists, and our country was founded upon creationist principles built around laws which were the laws of that Creator.

Our early schools — not only religious schools, but also public schools — taught creation when they first were established. But it wasn't long before Unitarians such as Horace Mann and others got control of the public school system. And it wasn't too long after that when John Dewey came along and established evolutionary humanism as the quasi-official religion of our public school system. With others of like mind, he formed the American Humanist Association with its humanist tenets. Since that time, our nation and its schools, its courts, its media, and just about our whole society, have been taken over by the evolutionary world view. Nevertheless, the creationist world view was really the foundation of our country.

The same thing is true with respect to science. True science does not support evolution; almost all of the founding fathers of science were creationists. Many people think that science came out of the Renaissance, but it did not. It was Greek evolutionary philosophy, which was restored in the Renaissance. True science came out of the Reformation when people began to have access to the Bible and were able to read and propagate the Word of God. This was true of the great early scientists such as Johannes Kepler, Isaac Newton, Robert Boyle, Pascal, Pasteur, Brewster, and most of the other great founding fathers of science. Almost without exception, these men were Bible-believing theists, who at least professed to believe in creation and in Christianity. Some might have been unorthodox in various ways, but they all believed in God as the Creator. They believed in the Bible, they believed in Christ, and many said — men such as Newton, Kepler, and Clerk Maxwell — that they were simply thinking God's thoughts after Him as they were doing their science. But now science has largely been taken over by the evolutionary world view. Our scientific establishment is currently circulating the idea that evolution is a proven fact of science, and everything has to be taught in the light of evolutionism. The fact is, however, that true science and true Americanism are all based on the foundation of special creation. The same is true of real biblical Christianity.

Jesus Christ as Creator

Sometimes we hear people say, "Don't get too involved in preaching creation. Just preach the gospel. What is important is to get people saved, not to make creationists out of them."

In a sense, we creationists would agree with that. But we need to realize that Jesus Christ was Creator before He became the Savior. The reason we even *need* a Savior is because we have rebelled against our Creator, who is Jesus Christ. "For by him were all things created, that are in heaven, and that are in earth, visible and invisible, whether they be thrones or dominions, or principalities or powers: all things were created by him" (Col. 1:16). "In the beginning was the Word, and the Word was with God, and the Word was God. The same was in the beginning with God. All things were made by him; and without him was not anything made that was made" (John 1:1–3). He is our Creator, and we don't really preach Christ without preaching Him as He really is. We don't want to preach "another Jesus" (2 Cor. 11:4). We want to preach Christ as He is. He is our Creator and our Savior and our coming King and Lord. That is the full scope of the gospel of Christ, and it is founded upon Christ as Creator.

In reference to Christ's saving gospel, the last and climactic time the word "gospel" is used in the Bible is in Revelation 14:6–7, where John says: "I saw another angel fly in the midst of heaven, having the everlasting gospel to preach unto them that dwell on the earth . . . Saying, with a loud voice, Fear God, and give glory to him; for the hour of his judgment is come, and worship him that made heaven, and earth, and the sea, and the fountains of waters." That's the final time (of the 101 times) where the word translated "gospel" is used in the New Testament.

Remember that Paul, in Galatians 1:8, said, in effect, that even though "an angel from heaven preach any other gospel unto you than that which we have preached unto you, let him be accursed." Therefore, we can be sure that this angel of Revelation 14 will be preaching the same gospel that Paul preached and the essence of the angel's gospel is a command to worship Him who had made heaven and earth and the sea and the fountains of waters. In other words, worshiping a Jesus who supposedly comes into our experience merely through some personal feeling, isn't the way it must be. We have to recognize that Jesus Christ is the Creator of the heavens and the earth, and all things therein. In Adam, we have all rebelled against Him and He has pronounced an age-long curse on the creation because of man's sin. Death has come in because of that; therefore, we need a Savior, and the great Creator is the only one who is able to be our Savior.

There are only two other nominally creationist religions besides Christianity — Islam and Judaism. They are creationist because they accept the Book of Genesis as their foundational account of creation. But then they refuse to acknowledge that the Creator must be the Savior, and that He must die and rise again in order to implement His purpose in creation. They hope wrongly that they can save themselves. Biblical Trinitarian Christianity is thus the only truly creationist religion. It is basic and essential that we *must* believe in creation and in the God of the Bible as Creator.

We could easily show that all the other basic doctrines of Christianity are also founded upon the doctrine of creation. A man once wrote me and said, "You shouldn't be talking about creation being the foundation, because Christ is the foundation of the Church." Yes, Christ the *Creator* is the foundation of the Church. And furthermore, He is the foundation of the whole creation, not just of the Church. He is the author, the finisher, the head, the Alpha and Omega, of everything. We need to preach Him as He really is.

On the other hand, the evolutionist world view tries to explain everything in terms of an eternal cosmos which never was created, never had a creator. The cosmos, itself, therefore, is the ultimate reality. That's basically what evolution is: it seeks to explain everything in terms of the cosmos and its processes, systems, and properties, even though these may sometimes be personified in terms of different gods and goddesses. Basically, it identifies ultimate reality with this physical universe. That evolutionary world view has come to dominate not only our modern world, but it has actually dominated the whole world since time began.

As far as the present order of things is concerned, I want to quote a statement from Sir Julian Huxley, who was probably the world's top evolutionist of the 20th century. He was the first director general of UNESCO, the main founder of neo-Darwinism, and, along with John Dewey, one of the chief founders of the American Humanist Association. Having written many, many books, Huxley was a profoundly influential scientist. In one of his articles, he said:

> The concept of evolution was soon extended into other than biological fields. Inorganic subjects, such as the life history of stars and the formation of the chemical elements on the one hand, and on the other hand, subjects like linguistics, social anthropology, and comparative law and religion are studied now from an evolutionary angle until today we are able to see evolution as a universal, all-pervading process.[2]

In another place, he said:

> The whole of reality is evolution, a single process of self-transformation.[3]

So every subject, not just biology and the natural sciences, but the social sciences, the fine arts, and other subjects today are taught within the framework of an evolutionary premise in our colleges, universities, public schools, and unfortunately, even in many Christian schools. Evolution is a world view which impacts every field, no matter what one's field of study may be.

I mentioned the American Humanist Association. Humanism is the religion that is really being taught in our public schools today. Now most secular authorities would not acknowledge that humanism is a religion, though some of them do. But basically, evolutionary humanism is a very religious point of view. The tenets of the American Humanist Association, which were promulgated primarily by John Dewey, Julian Huxley, and others of like mind back when they formed the organization in 1933, really provide what we find being taught in our schools and also in the news media today. Whether explicit or not, these tenets of humanism have become the quasi-official doctrine of our intellectual world. The original tenets of humanism set forth in 1933 were combined with another manifesto in 1973 and published by the American Humanist Association in the magazine *The Humanist*. In his preface, Editor Paul Kurtz said:

> Humanism is a philosophical, religious, and moral point of view as old as human civilization itself. . . . It has its roots in classical China, Greece, and Rome; it is expressed in the Renaissance and the Enlightenment, in the scientific revolution, and in the twentieth century.[4]

Humanism: A Denial of God

And what is humanism? Its first tenet is that "religious humanists regard the universe as self-existing and not created." This first tenet holds that there was no creation; the universe is the ultimate reality. It is self-existing. The second tenet of humanism states that "man is a part of nature and he had emerged as a result of a continuous process."[5] There is no Creator, there is no creation; everything is explained in terms of evolution. The other humanist tenets involve a world government, complete freedom of sex, and all of the other things that we see causing so much havoc in society today. The late Isaac Asimov, who was president of the American Humanist Association and one of the most prolific science writers of our time, was a bitter opponent of creationism. He refused to debate any creationist scientist publicly, but he wrote against creationism vigorously in his publications. Asimov, who is said to have produced more than 500 books covering every field of science, probably knew science as well as anybody. What he said, in case you have any questions about what humanism really is: "I am an atheist, out and out." Humanism is basically an esoteric form of atheism. He went on to say:

> Emotionally, I'm an atheist — I don't have
> the evidence to prove that God doesn't exist. But
> I so strongly suspect He doesn't that I don't want
> to waste my time.[6]

Now if anybody would have any scientific evidence against God, it would seem that Isaac Asimov would. But he admitted that he didn't; and if he didn't, then nobody does.

So people are not evolutionists because of science; scientific evidence does not support evolution. If anybody maintains that it does, just challenge them, "Well, show me the scientific proof." Science is supposed to be what you can see, but no one has ever seen any evolution take place. As long as people have been looking at changes in biological organisms, no one has ever seen a new species evolve. No one has ever seen a new star evolve. No one has ever seen evolution from simple to complex take place anywhere in the whole universe in all human history, and nobody knows how evolution works to this very day.

Charles Darwin became famous 140 years ago by solving that problem, the humanists thought, with his *Origin of Species by Natural Selection*. However, Dr. Colin

Patterson of England, a great evolutionist, has said, in effect, that no one has ever seen a new species come into existence by natural selection. [7] Nobody knows how it works; nobody has ever seen it happen. If we go to the fossil record, there are no evolutionary transitional forms there, either. Evolution is even contrary to the laws of thermodynamics, the basic laws of science. There is no scientific evidence for evolution whatsoever. People don't believe in evolution because of science. In spite of science, they believe in evolution because emotionally they don't want to believe in God.

Now a concept which is based on the rejection of the very possibility of a God who created and now controls His cosmos is bound to create havoc in the world. Charles Darwin ended his famous book, *The Origin of Species by Natural Selection*, like this:

> Thus, from the war of nature, from famine and death, the most exalted object which we are capable of conceiving, namely the production of the higher animals, [by which he means man] directly follows.[8]

In other words, man came about by suffering and death. Suffering and death are basically good things because they produce evolution. The struggle for existence, survival of the fittest, natural selection — that's the ultimate good in the world.

But that's exactly opposite to what God has said in His Word. Darwin says, "By death came man." The Bible says, "By man came death" (1 Cor. 15:21). There was no death, suffering, or struggle for existence in the world until sin came into it via man. God then had to pronounce the curse on the whole creation, which had been given to man as his dominion. Because of this introduction of spiritual disorder, God pronounced His judgment of physical disorder on man's dominion, and there has been suffering and death in the world ever since then. And, as we shall see, a philosophy which says suffering and death are good because they produce evolution is bound to become a *cause* of death itself.

Stephen J. Gould, the most articulate modern evolutionist, has insisted in many of his writings, in one way or another, that "evolution is a proved fact of science." This is a litany that evolutionists repeat over and over, as if they expect everybody to believe it because they say it so often. But then when people ask Gould for evidence that proves evolution, he says that the best evidence for evolution is imperfection in the universe. For example, he cites the panda's thumb, which he says could have been designed better, if he or some engineer had designed it. Imperfections in the animal world, he says, prove that God didn't have anything to do with creation because God would make everything perfect.[9]

However, the fact that God *made* everything perfect doesn't mean it's going to *stay* perfect! We do have the reality of sin in the world, and mutations, disease, decay, disintegration, and death because of sin. But rather than proving evolution, these imperfections really prove that we are alienated from God because of sin. Evolutionists have to become apologists for suffering and death if such things supposedly contribute to evolution. So Fascists promote nazism and Marxists promote communism (Gould himself is a Marxist), because they are supposed to advance evolution.

Evolution's Destructive Impact

This idea of struggle for existence and survival of the fittest has had a terrible impact on the world as a whole. For example, laissez-faire capitalism became the watchword of England, America, Germany, and the Western world back in the 19th century. Even many of our conservative political people today still endorse evolution because they think that the survival of the fittest applies in society and in economics today. But we need to realize that all of this was based on evolution, too. For example, the great steel baron, Andrew Carnegie, whom we tend to honor because of his charitable endowments, said,

> [The law of competition] is here; we can-not evade it; no substitutes for it have been found; and while the law may sometimes be hard for the individual, it is best for the race, because it insures the survival of the fittest in every de-partment.[10]

So let's exploit labor, let's do whatever we have to do to advance capitalism. What's good for the corporation is good for the world. Here's what Carnegie said in his auto-biography:

> I remember that the light came in as a flood and all was clear. Not only had I gotten rid of theology and the supernatural, but I had found the truth of evolution.[11]

That was the basis for his actions. John D. Rockefeller said much the same thing, and so did Raymond Hill, the railroad baron. In fact, all the great "robber barons" of the 19th century, as many called them, were basically fol-lowing Herbert Spencer, particularly with his "survival of the fittest" concept. Spencer even opposed child labor laws because he believed only the fittest should survive, and that's what would contribute to the advancement of society.

Of course, in Germany, the concept of "survival of the fittest" led finally to World War I and later to the ex-treme racist philosophies of Hitlerism and World War II. Let me pass along just one statement from an authority, Daniel Gasmann, who said of Adolf Hitler in his book *The Scientific Origins of National Socialism:*

> (Hitler) stressed and singled out the idea of biological evolution as the most forceful weapon against traditional religion and he repeatedly condemned Christianity for its opposition to the teachings of evolution. . . . Hitler was a strong evolutionist — for Hitler, evolution was the hallmark of modern science and culture.[12]

He was also an occultist who was committed to astrology. But basically, he was a Darwinian and an evolutionist and he felt that in the struggle for existence among nations, the greater nations would survive. So it was justified in his mind to wage that kind of war. Even in England, Sir Arthur Keith, a leading evolutionary anthropologist acknowledged that Hitler was a good evolutionist and that he was following the principles of evolution in his plans for the war.

Communism also is based on evolution. And racism is completely based on evolution. All the great evolutionary scientists of the 19th century were evolutionary racists, including Charles Darwin. In his book *The Descent of Man*, Darwin stressed that there was an ascending order of evolution among the races. Thomas Huxley said the same thing. In fact, essentially all evolutionary scientists of the 19th century were racists.

The same thing applied, particularly among the anthropologists, even up to the mid-20th century. Men such as Henry Fairfield Osborn, the director of the American Museum of Natural History, believed that the Negro race, for example, was not even of the same species as *Homo sapiens*. These men of science said some terrible things about the supposed "lower races." Of course, with World War II and Hitler's genocide and racist activities, racism lost favor among scientists and most evolutionary scientists today have given up these most racist views.

What about all the social practices we're so alarmed

about today, such as the drug culture, abortion, pornography, immorality, and others? If space permitted, we could document that all of these are based on evolutionary philosophy.

That doesn't necessarily mean that, for example, every young woman who has an abortion or doctor who performs one is an evolutionist. People commit sin for all kinds of reasons. But whenever anybody tries to rationalize these things on a scientific basis, they fall back on evolutionism as their rationale.

For example, take a look at this quote reported in the *Los Angeles Times* from Elie A. Schneour, the director of the Biosystems Research Institute in La Jolla, California, and chairman of the Southern California Skeptics, an affiliate of the American Association for the Advancement of Science. Quoting Schneour:

> Ontogeny recapitulates phylogeny. This is a fundamental tenet of modern biology that derives from evolutionary theory and is thus anathema to creationism as well as to those opposed to freedom of choice. Ontogeny is the name for the process of development of a fertilized egg into a fully formed and mature living organism. Phylogeny, on the other hand, is the history of the evolution of a species, in this case, the human being. During development, the fertilized egg progresses over 38 weeks through what is, in fact, a rapid passage through evolutionary history. From a single, primordial cell, the conceptus progresses through being something of a protozoan, a fish, a reptile, a bird, a primate, and ultimately a human being. [13]

Thus, the justification some people use for killing a fetus in the womb is that it isn't really human. If people who propose freedom of choice and abortion really believed that this was a human being, then they would have to acknowledge that killing it is murder. But they don't believe it's a human being. Their rationale for saying that is to say that it is merely going through its evolutionary history.

But the fact is that this recapitulation theory, this so-called biogenetic law, was disproved at least 50 years ago, and no knowledgeable biologist or embryologist would still believe in the recapitulation theory. It is completely unscientific. The embryo never does go through a fish stage. It never has gills or a tail or anything like that. In fact, the DNA which programs the whole development indicates that the embryo is a human being right from the very time of conception. There's no rationale whatever, in terms of real science, to support the idea that it ever is anything but a human being.

As with abortion, it would be possible to show that all these harmful practices basically find their rationale in evolutionism. We could show that to be true of our modern drug culture, for example. Aldous Huxley, Timothy Leary, and the others who were the founding fathers of the modern emphasis on drugs some 50 years or so ago, said in effect that although evolution has proved there is no God, we still need some kind of religious experience. Aldous Huxley then said that we could compress an eternity of joy into just a few hours with the materials that the pharmacologists provide for us.[14] The drug culture is based on the rejection of God because of evolution.

New Age Seduction

What about the New Age movement? The New Age movement, in all of its multiplicity and complexity, encompasses witchcraft and astrology and spiritism on the one hand, and the anthropic principal and biosystems and biogenetic fields and so forth on the other hand. Many churches, cultures, and religions now are involved in some aspect or other of the New Age movement. All such New Age cults and movements have two main features in common:

1) their goal is a world culture, a world religion, a world government; and
2) they base their world view, without exception, on some form of evolution.

The "patron saint" of the New Age movement seems to be the Jesuit priest Teilhard de Chardin. Marilyn Ferguson, who wrote *The Aquarian Conspiracy,* the so-called bible of the New Age movement, polled most of the leaders of the movement asking them who had been the most influential person in leading them to their philosophical position. By far, most of them answered de Chardin.

And what was his view? Here's what he says in his book, *The Phenomenon of Man:*

> Is evolution a theory, a system, or a hypothesis? It is much more: it is a general condition to which all theories, all systems, all hypotheses must bow and which they must satisfy henceforward if they are to be thinkable and true. Evolution is a light illuminating all facts, a curve that all lines must follow.[15]

Evolution, to him, was God. Only it was not a personal god, but a god of nature, a pantheistic god. And, of course, the New Age orbit in general is essentially a restoration of ancient pantheism. It sounds a little bit more spiritual to say "pantheism," which means "all god," or "god is everywhere," than it does to say "atheism," which means "no god." But, if God really is everywhere in general, then He is nowhere in particular. There is really no difference between pantheism and atheism in terms of the practicality of God's existence and meaning.

People will ask, "But wasn't de Chardin a Catholic

priest? Didn't he believe in Christ?" Yes, he did. But listen to what he said about Jesus Christ. "It is Christ, in very truth, who saves — but should we not immediately add that at the same time it is Christ who is saved by evolution."[16]

Evolution is, thus, not only the creator but also the savior, and now that we understand past evolution, we can control future evolution, so he thought. And as the Humanist Manifesto of 1973 says, "No deity will save us; we will save ourselves." A former assistant secretary general of the United Nations, Robert Muller, who is currently one of the leaders of the New Age movement, has said, "The most fundamental thing we can do today is to believe in evolution."[17] He has said, in effect, that our whole system must be based on evolution if we are to realize the utopian goal of world government.

Thus, the impact of evolution today is worldwide and it is devastatingly harmful everywhere. I don't think we could find a single good product that has come out of evolutionary philosophy. It hasn't produced any scientific discoveries or new inventions or a higher standard of living. Evolutionary theory doesn't produce anything good in science, yet it's considered to be the basic premise in science by many scientists. Amazing!

But, where did this evolutionary paradigm come from? Most people think that it came from Charles Darwin's *Origin of Species*. Yes, Darwin was a catalyst who was tremendously influential, both in his day and in our day. He changed the world in a very real way. Yet he didn't invent evolutionism. As a matter of fact, he didn't even discover the idea of natural selection. In my own reading, I have found that at least 11 men had published books or articles advocating natural selection before Charles Darwin did. In fact, Darwin's grandfather, Erasmus Darwin, did so before Charles was even born. Benjamin Franklin believed in natural selection. And so did various others.

But the most influential person in this area was a man

by the name of Alfred Russel Wallace. I must tell you a little about him because it does seem more than coincidental that the time when modern Darwinian evolution was coming to the fore back in the mid-19th century was also the time when ancient witchcraft, spiritism, and occultism, (of which Wallace was a leading advocate) were being revived in the Western world. These practices had always been prominent in the world of pantheism in other nations and in the ethnic religions of the world, but in the western "scientific" world, spiritism and occultism only began to be revived about the same time as Darwinian evolution began to be promoted, and Wallace was right in the middle of it. Before I continue his story, however, a little more background is needed.

I mentioned earlier that a long war has been raging between Satan and God. Perhaps it was because of the God-sent revivals and the Christian world view that dominated Victorian England and our own nation in its early days, and the worldwide missions programs going out from their shores, Satan determined to accelerate his war with our Almighty God. Three men of this period are generally believed to have had the greatest influence on modern thought:

1) Sigmund Freud, in the field of psychology and human relationships;
2) Karl Marx, in the field of economics and political science; and
3) Charles Darwin, in the field of natural science.

These men all seem to have had some strange occult influences behind what they were doing.

Scholar Paul Vitz, in his book *Sigmund Freud and His Christian Unconscious*,[18] gives an abundance of evidence that Sigmund Freud (whom most people believe to have been an atheist, but who really was a pantheist) based his system on the (now discredited) recapitulation theory. Vitz explains that Freud thought that people have psychological hang-ups because they haven't evolved far enough; therefore, he argued, they can be treated by psychoanalysis. Vitz says that Freud was very much preoccupied with things like the devil, antichrist, demonism, and so forth, and then he presents some rather significant evidence that Freud might even have made a Faustian pact with the devil. Incidentally, his contemporary, psychologist Carl Jung, was a convinced and practicing spiritist.

The same thing has been shown to be true of Karl Marx. In his book *Marx and Satan*, Richard Wurmbrand suggests that Karl Marx was not just an atheist as we tend to think. Marx had been a professing Christian through high school. In fact, he wrote a rather interesting essay that appeared in *Christianity Today* many years ago on "Abiding in Christ." It sounded like a spiritual testimony from a pious young Christian talking about how important it was to abide in Christ. But shortly after that essay was published, he, like Freud, seems to have made some kind of Faustian pact with the devil. He even says in one of his poems, "My goal is to destroy him who reigns above." Wurmbrand makes a strong case for the belief that Marx was actually a Satanist.[19]

As far as Darwin was concerned, he wasn't a Satanist or occultist; he was an atheist, although there may be some rather equivocal evidence that he had a partial change in his thinking near the end of his life. At any rate, up until very near the time of his death, Darwin was an atheist who occasionally wavered between being an atheist and an agnostic. He firmly rejected Christianity, the Bible, and creation.

He had been working on his theory of natural selection for some 20 years there in England, ever since he returned from his well-known, round-the-world voyage on the *Beagle*. He was being influenced by Sir Charles Lyell, in particular, to try to develop and publish this theory. But Darwin was afraid to publish it; he didn't think he had enough evidence, so he kept looking for more evidence, with the intention of eventually publishing a massive tome on natural selection. But all of a sudden, he quickly condensed his material and got his book out, because he was afraid he was going to be pre-empted by none other than the openly occultic Alfred Russel Wallace.

Wallace was an interesting person. He was an anarchist and a "spiritualist." In fact, he was one of the leaders in the spiritist revival in England at the time. He wrote books and articles on the scientific evidence for spiritism and he believed that one could communicate with the spirits, just like modern New Age people believe they can do through what they call "channeling." Furthermore, Wallace had spent many, many years in the jungles, working with animistic tribes who also believed in communication with the spirits. Wallace thought very highly of these people; he did not agree with Darwin, who thought they were primitive people, just a little above the apes. He thought very highly of them because he had worked with them and knew they were true and intelligent human beings. In fact, he would not go along with Darwin's idea that man's soul had evolved as well as his body. He believed that some sort of a pantheistic, cosmic consciousness had generated man's soul. Wallace was a self-educated man who had never had much opportunity to associate with the scientists of England — he had only met Darwin and Lyell very briefly, but he knew that they were interested in the origin of the species, as he was.

Wallace later wrote this testimony in a book called *The Wonderful Century*:

> I was then (February 1858) living at Ternate in the Moluccas, and was suffering from a rather severe attack of intermittent fever, which prostrated me every day during the cold and succeeding hot fits. During one of these fits, while again considering the problem of the ori-

gin of species, something led me to think of Malthus' *Essay on Population.*

Malthus had written about the survival of the fittest in human populations and he had been quite influential in Darwin's thinking, too. Wallace continued:

> The whole method of species modification became clear to me, and in the two hours of my fit, I had thought out the main points of the theory. That same evening, I sketched out the draft of a paper; and in the two succeeding evenings, I wrote it out and sent it by the next post to Mr. Darwin.[20]

When he received the draft, Darwin was astounded. He told his friend, Lyell, that Wallace had anticipated everything that he had poured 20 years of research into in preparation for his big book. So Darwin had to come out with a book right away in order to establish priority. He never did publish his big book, and probably never would have published a book at all had it not been for Wallace sending him this information, stating that he had discovered the theory, not like Darwin, during 20 years of research among the leading scientists in England, but during two hours of a fit in the Malaysian jungles. Loren Eiseley, a great historian of science at the University of Pennsylvania, said in an article about Wallace:

> A man pursuing birds of paradise in a remote jungle did not yet know that he had forced the world's most reluctant author to disgorge his hoarded volume, or that the whole of Western thought was about to be swung into a new channel because a man in a fever had felt a moment of strange radiance.[21]

I cannot help thinking that there is more to all this than meets the eye. This may well have been the beginning of the modern strategy in Satan's long war.

Evolutionists before Darwin

But then, of course, neither Wallace nor Darwin originated evolution. As we go back to consider men before Darwin (his grandfather, Erasmus, for example, and other leading evolutionists), we find all sorts of strange influences being brought to bear on them.

Various German "nature philosophers," and various French philosophers had all been influenced very much by a system called the "great chain of being." This concept is not taught much anymore, but the ancient idea of a great chain of being was that there was a continual link between all orders of reality in the cosmos. This is not a biblical concept, but it does have sort of a religious flavor. It starts out with the divine essence, whatever that may be. Some of the medieval religionists put that into the form of the theological God, but that wasn't the way it started out. It was just the divine essence of nature. That developed somehow down in a continual link through the spirit world — angels, demons, whatever other spirits there might have been — down to the highest races of human beings, then down to the lower races, then to the great apes, then to the other animals, then to the insects, then to the nonliving things, and finally down to the elementary particles. The idea was that there was a chain of being in which there were no missing links; it was up to the philosophers and scientists to discover them.

Of course, all that the 19th century evolutionists had to do was to invert this chain of being and then put a time scale on it to come up with the modern evolutionary system. That chain of being was really the basis for the early studies of comparative anatomy and comparative embryology. The idea was that everything had to go through this chain from simple to complex or complex to simple. So the development of the embryo progresses from very simple to complex. Their comparative anatomy had to be based on the idea of studying and comparing the simplest organisms on up to the most complex. Finally, when it came time to develop a geological time scale (there is no place in the world where the complete standard geological column is ever found except in a text book), it was developed by assuming that the simple forms of life had to be early in the chain of being and the more complex forms of life later. That was imposed on the study of paleontology, and was finally built up into our standard geological time scale. Thus, the recapitulation theory in embryology, the geological column, the idea of races being inferior and superior, and the idea of human beings not having fully developed and therefore still having psychological hang-ups — all these things were based ultimately on this idea of the great chain of being.

And where did that come from? Not from the Bible, obviously. It came from the ancient philosophers, probably mostly from Plato. But it became most prominently expressed among the neo-Platonists after the time of Christ.

Ancient Greek philosophers, without exception, were evolutionists. Even though some believed in a sort of god, a prime mover, or some great force behind it all, they did not believe there was a personal Creator/God who had created the universe. They all believed that the universe was the ultimate reality and that it had gradually expressed itself in terms of the chain of being. Paul dealt with some of them, as recorded in Acts 17. The Epicureans were atheists; the Stoics were pantheists. There were also many varieties of Gnostics, but they were all pantheists, though some of them tried to mix Christianity with their Gnostic pantheism, when Christianity became prominent.

In fact, one can trace such beliefs on back through Plato and Socrates and then even to the pre-Socratic philosophers back around 600 B.C. in Greece. Among these were such men as Thales, Anaximander, and Anaximenes, as well as later thinkers such as Leucippus, Democritus, and others who developed a completely materialistic philosophy, an evolutionary system which became prominent in Greece and later in Rome. Evolution is not a modern idea at all!

But where did the Greeks learn it?According to Milton Munitz, professor of the philosophy of science at New York University and one of the greatest authorities on the history of science:

> Anaximander reinterprets, while at the same time retaining, basically the same pattern of cosmogonical development that is to be found in the Babylonian myth, as this had already been partly transformed in the Greek version of Hesiod's theogony.[22]

Homer and Hesiod had taught a polytheistic system of gods and goddesses, but really, polytheism is just a form of pantheism. Pantheism is the all-god, expressed locally as the god of fire, the god of thunder, the goddess of the river, and so forth. The forces of nature personified altogether represent the all-god, the whole cosmic consciousness, or Mother Earth, Gaia, or Mother Nature. They got all this, Munitz says, from Babylon.

But now we have to think in biblical terms, because reliable secular history does not go further back than this. It is significant that the Bible says that Babylon the Great is the mother of harlots and abominations of the earth. Once we get back into that era, long before 1000 B.C. which was Hesiod's time, we've stepped into the realm of mythology, except for the Bible. We don't have any genuine recorded history from that far back except what we find in the Bible and a few archaeological monuments.

Many people don't want to go to the Bible for their information, of course, but that's where the best information is.The Book of Genesis, in chapters 10 and 11, tells us that Babel was the center of the first great world kingdom and that Nimrod was its founder. The beginning of his kingdom was Babel, but Nimrod also founded Nineveh and other great cities. He was the first great world emperor.

He was the great-grandson of Noah, so he was living not very long after the Flood. It had probably been at least 100 years or so, however, enough time to build a fairly good population, since people were still living for hundreds of years. But instead of going out and filling the earth like God had told them, Nimrod wanted to make a name for himself and his people. So they decided to build a great city and a great tower — not to *reach* "unto heaven," but rather, to be dedicated unto the heavens, to the host of heaven, to the angels, to the stars. (The stars and the angels are frequently mentioned almost interchangeably in the Bible. Stars are called angels and angels are called stars frequently, because everything in the realm of the heavens where the stars are is also where the angels are.)

This tower dedicated to the host of heaven probably had at its apex a great shrine with the zodiac symbols emblazoned on its walls. But God then came down and confused their languages and scattered the people across the face of the earth. They couldn't talk to each other anymore, so each little family group became isolated and segregated. The family groups eventually developed into nations, some of which became extinct (e.g. the Neanderthals), others developed into great kingdoms such as Egypt and Sumeria, and some continued indefinitely as "primitive" societies.

It is significant that the Babylonian origins myth, the Egyptian origins myth, and the cosmogonies of many other nations around the world, exhibit a rather amazing similarity. Although the tribes scattered from Babel couldn't talk to each other anymore, they all carried the same religion with them everywhere. They adopted different names for their gods and goddesses, corresponding to their different languages. But basically the same system of evolutionary religion — pantheistic, humanistic, astrological, spiritistic — was carried everywhere and the source of all this was, apparently, the Babylonian cosmogony. That cosmogony was the *Enuma Elish*. This famous Babylonian "genesis" said that originally there was nothing but a watery chaos everywhere and out of this watery chaos two gods just appeared, and from them everything else came. One finds the same thing in Egypt, the same thing in Hesiod, in many of the African tribes and American Indian tribes, this idea of a primal chaos. But none of them tell where the creation, the universe, came from. All start with the universe in a chaotic condition, usually a watery chaos.

That immediately makes us think of Genesis, of course, where, "In the beginning, God created the heaven and the earth. And the earth was without form, and void; and darkness was upon the face of the deep. And the Spirit of God moved upon the face of the waters. And God said let there be light" (Gen. 1:1–3).

Initially, there was water everywhere. It wasn't chaos; it was all perfect for that particular stage of God's created work. God created the angels as well as human beings. Angels were created first, probably on the first day of creation, and Satan was the highest of all the angels, as we read in Ezekiel 28:15–17. He was perfect in his ways and full of wisdom and perfect in brightness and beauty until iniquity was found in him and God told him that He was going to cast him to the earth. Everything was "very good" at the end of the six days of creation (Gen. 1:31), so it was after that when God cast Satan to the earth. He had said, in effect, "I want to exalt my throne above the stars of God, I want to be God. I want to ascend above the Most High" (Isa. 14:13–14). In other words, he thinks he is of the same order as God.[23] Then Satan tempted Adam and Eve, apparently with the same temptation with which he had tempted himself, saying they could be like gods.

Now where would he get such an absurd idea? When he first came into existence, all he knew was that God told him that he had been created for a great purpose, but all he could see was this watery "chaos" around him. That's where he was when he was created, and all the other angels had been created the same way. So he thought perhaps, that he was of the same order as God, and God had just arrived a bit before him. It might be just a matter of time before he could successfully rebel and become God himself or, at least, like God. So he, at that time, initiated his long war against God. Now if Satan (or Lucifer) is going to believe that God isn't really the Creator, then he has to have some other explanation. That's why I have to believe that Satan was the first evolutionist. Evolutionists may scoff at such an idea, but again, I can think of no better explanation for how this worldwide, age-long lie came to be, than through the father of liars, who is the devil. Satan is the deceiver of the whole world, but he has deceived himself most of all! And he still thinks, apparently — because he is still fighting against God — that somehow he is going to win. So he keeps on fighting. He has to use the same lie with which he deceived himself, that the universe is the ultimate reality, that it is evolving itself into higher and higher systems, and that now men think they can even control its future evolution.

We who believe in the Bible know that's not the way it's going to end. But that's the way it looks right now. And it looks like Satan is getting control pretty rapidly. God's Word does say that we "wrestle not against flesh and blood, but against principalities, against powers, against the rulers of the darkness of this world, against spiritual wickedness in high places" (Eph. 6:12).

Therefore, we cannot fight this war with bullets or even with ballots. "Though we walk in the flesh, we do not war after the flesh; (For the weapons of our warfare are not carnal, but mighty through God, to the pulling down of strongholds), casting down imaginations, and every high thing that exalteth itself against the knowledge of God, and bringing into captivity every thought to the obedience of Christ" (2 Cor. 10:3–5).

That's our commission, to fight that war. It is a spiritual battle. We have to have the girdle of truth and the breastplate of righteousness and the helmet of salvation and our feet shod with the gospel of peace. We must have the shield of faith, and the sword of the spirit, which is the Word of God, and all this weaponry must be accompanied by a great aura of prayer (Eph. 6:14-18); then the weapons are powerful and mighty through God to the pulling down of strongholds.

Finally, we can read in the Book of Revelation how it's all going to come out. There it says that all the kings in the world one day are going to give their allegiance to the great humanist man who gives his allegiance to Satan. They are all going to worship the beast, as this man of sin is called, and they are going to worship the dragon who gave his power to the beast. The whole world will become Satanists then, and all the kings of the earth are going to give their power to him. They are all going to "make war with the Lamb, but the Lamb shall overcome them: for he is Lord of lords and King of kings; and they that are with him are called, and chosen, and faithful" (Rev. 17:14).

It's going to be better to be with Him than with them in that day!

Endnotes

1   For documentation of the strong Christian and biblical background of our nation, one can refer to the following books, among others: *Faith of Our Founding Fathers* by Tim LaHaye (Master Books); *Christianity and the Constitution* by John Eidsmoe (Baker Book House); and *The Myth of Separation* by David Barton (Wall Builder Press).

2   J.R. Newman, editor, *What is Science?*, "Evolution and Genetics," by Sir Julian Huxley (New York, NY: Simon and Schuster, 1955), p. 272.

3   Ibid., p. 278.

4   Paul Kurtz, Preface to "Humanist Manifesto II," *The Humanist,* vol. 33 (September/October 1973): p. 2.

5 American Humanist Association, "Humanist Manifesto," *The New Humanist,* vol. 6 (May/June 1933).

6 Paul Kurtz, "An Interview with Isaac Asimov on Science and the Bible," *Free Inquiry,* vol. 2 (Spring 1982): p. 9.

7 Colin Patterson, "Cladistics," interview by Brian Leek, interviewer Peter Franz, B.B.C., March 4, 1982.

8 Charles Darwin, *Origin of Species,* last paragraph, 1859.

9 Stephen J. Gould; see, for example, "Darwinism Defined," *Discover* (January 1987): p. 68.

10 Richard Hofstadter, *Social Darwinism in American Thought* (Boston, MA:Beacon Press, 1955), p. 41, citing Andrew Carnegie, "Wealth," *North American Review,* 148 (1889).

11 Ibid., p. 45, citing Andrew Carnegie, *Autobiography of Andrew Carnegie,* (Boston, MA: Houghton-Mifflin Company, 1920).

12 Daniel Gasmann, *The Scientific Origins of National Socialism* (New York, NY: American Elsevier, 1971), p. 168.

13 Elie A. Scheour, "Life Doesn't Begin, It Continues," *Los Angeles Times,* January 29, 1989, part 5, p. 5.

14 Aldous Huxley, "History of Tension," *Scientific Monthly,* vol. 85 (July 1957): p. 9.

15 Teilhard de Chardin, *The Phenomenon of Man* (New York, NY: Harper and Row, 1965), p. 219.

16 Teilhard de Chardin, *The Heart of the Matter* (New York, NY: Harcourt, Brace, Jovanovich, 1979), p. 92.

17 Kristin Murphy, "United Nations' Robert Muller," *The Movement Newsletter* (September 1983): p. 10, citing Robert Muller.

18 Paul Vitz, *Sigmund Freud and His Christian Unconscious* (New York, NY: Guilford Press, 1988).

19 Richard Wurmbrand, *Marx and Satan* (Westchester, IL: Crossway Books, 1987), p. 143.

20 Alfred Russel Wallace, *The Wonderful Century* (New York, NY, 1898), p. 139–140.

21 Loren Eisely, "Alfred Russel Wallace," *Scientific American,* vol. 200 (February 1959): p. 81.

22 Milton K. Munitz, *Space, Time and Creation* (Glencoe, IL: The Free Press, 1957), p. 67.

23 For a more complete and comprehensive discussion of this great conflict of the ages, see the writer's book, *The Long War Against God* (Green Forest, AR: Master Books, 2000).

Chapter 2

BIBLICAL AUTHORITY AND THE BOOK OF GENESIS

Ken Ham

If I have told you earthly things, and ye believe not, how shall ye believe, if I tell you of heavenly things? (John 3:12; KJV).

Think about this verse very carefully, as I apply it in a particular way. If you can't trust the Bible when it talks about geology, biology, and astronomy, then how can you trust the Bible when it talks about morality and salvation? The issues of morality and salvation are dependent upon the history in the Bible being true. God does not separate morality and salvation from geology, biology, and astronomy. However, it's popular today for liberal scholars to claim that the Bible doesn't speak about science.

Now if we can't believe the Bible when it talks about earthly things — the rocks, the trees, and the animals and plants, then how can we believe the heavenly things (i.e., salvation) that are so important?

All of us, myself included, have been what I call

evolutionized. You might say that you don't believe in evolution; bear with me.

When we hear the word "evolution," it can mean many different things to many different people. We have to define what we mean by it. Evolution, in an ultimate sense, is more than a mechanism. It's a whole way of thinking, a philosophy of life that teaches that man, by himself, independent of God, determines truth. It's very important to understand that. Again, I believe we've all been evolutionized. Let me explain why.

We all go back to one man, Adam. We sin like Adam; Paul makes that very clear in Romans 5, for instance. As a result, all of us are going to have the same propensity that Adam had. We would rather listen to the words of fallible man than the Word of God. That's the bottom line. That was Adam's sin, wasn't it?

Now we all have that nature. This leads us to be so easily influenced by the fallible words of sinful men, who don't know everything, who weren't there, instead of listening to the Word of the infallible God, who knows everything, who's always been there.

Fallible men are trying to change the infallible Word of God. What I have come to recognize more and more is that if the Bible is a revelation from God to us, and if God has revealed the truth about the entire universe to enable us to understand who we are, what's happened, why we're here . . . then everything that He has revealed in His Word has to be foundational to all our thinking in every area.

Because the Bible *is* the infallible Word from the Creator God, it must be foundational to all of our thinking. But you see, we tend to take our ideas *to* the Bible. Our nature is such that we try to determine truth independently, by ourselves, and then add that to the Bible.

But we need to understand that Christianity is founded in history. In fact, I call the Bible the history book of the universe. Christianity is not a pie-in-the-sky religion. Christianity is based in real history. Think about it; if the events of Jesus Christ's birth, death, and resurrection didn't happen in history, how can we be saved? If we all don't go back to one man in history, a literal man in a literal garden, then who are we? Where did we come from?

As I travel around, sometimes I get so dejected when I talk to Christian leaders. A number of Christian leaders have told me recently, "Genesis is just a metaphor." I reply that if Genesis is a metaphor, then what about the account of Adam and Eve? Well, "It's a metaphor," they answer.

It's interesting to me that if we look up the genealogies in the Bible (e.g., Luke and Chronicles), something becomes quite clear: all the genealogies show that Jesus Christ was a descendant of Adam. So are we to believe that real people go back to real people . . . all the way back to a metaphor? In Jude, does Scripture say, "Enoch, the seventh from a metaphor"?

When I read my Bible, it has all these real people going back to a real person called Adam. Enoch was seventh from Adam. It's critical that we believe in the history of the Bible. Psalms tells us, "Thy Word is true from the beginning" (Ps. 119:160). If we don't believe it is real history, then who are we? Where did we come from? Why are we sinners? The history is foundational to understanding what Christianity is all about, and you see the importance of historical reality when you read through the Bible:

- A perfect creation is marred by sin, and death is a consequence.

- The catastrophe of Noah's flood, with geological changes around the globe, and biology on board the ark.

- As a result of the confusion at the Tower of Babel, when God gave different languages, the population splits up into different people groups that move out over the earth. This division results in different characteristics of people groups, depending on what collections of genes they have.

- Jesus Christ becomes a man of flesh and blood, He dies on a cross, and He is raised from the dead.

- One day there's going to be a new heaven and a new earth.

Here, then, is what's happened in history, while we are now waiting for eternity. We have to understand that this biblical history should be like a pair of glasses. As I say to people, when we look at the universe we should always have on our biblical glasses.

In a recent *Time* cover story, astronomers speculated on how the universe will end. They begin with evolutionary presuppositions, so the truth is that they really have no idea how the universe will end. Some say it will burn up, others claim it will freeze.

Peter, the apostle, tells us through revelation that even the elements will burn up one day, so that God can refashion the earth by purging it of its impurities. He will rid everything of the curse. *Time* magazine has it wrong.

I suggest that most people, even in our churches, have the wrong glasses on. We're wearing evolutionized glasses, and we're trying to add God to our evolutionized understanding, and we wonder why we have all sorts of problems. Let me give a practical example. One of the questions I get asked all the time is this: "How do you fit dinosaurs with the Bible?" Are you ready for a shock? I answer, "You don't fit dinosaurs with the Bible!"

Now why did I say that?

Well, you don't take man's interpretation of the evidence and try to fit dinosaurs into the Bible. Here's the point: you use the Bible to explain dinosaurs. You use the Bible as history, and put on your biblical glasses. Does the Bible tell us when God made land animals? Absolutely. Does He tell us what they ate before sin? Definitely! Does the Bible tell us anything about their history? Yes, they sailed on a boat. Where did they end up? In the Middle East. And then what? They came out of the boat. What happened to the dinosaurs that didn't get on the boat? They drowned. What would you expect to find? Dead ones. What do you find today in the fossil record? Dead ones.

So, what happened to the world's dinosaur population? Well, because of sin and the curse and the effects of the Flood, things are dying out; extinction is the rule (a number of species of animals become extinct every day). There is a very long list of animals that have become extinct, including dinosaurs. What, then, is the mystery? It's only a mystery if you take man's fallible interpretation of the evidence in the present and somehow try to fit it to the Bible. It is not a mystery if you accept the Bible as history — you already have the right way of thinking with which to understand the evidence.

By the way, the same approach works with the Grand Canyon. How do you fit the Grand Canyon into the Bible? You don't, but you use the Bible to explain the Grand Canyon. And that is a totally different way of thinking. Consider this: creationists and evolutionists, Christians and non-Christians, humanists and Christians — do we all study the same world? Of course! Do we have the same animals? Do we have the same fossils? Do we have the same Grand Canyon? The same universe? Do we have the same facts? Yes! The facts are all the same. What is the difference?

How you look at the facts.

In other words, the fight is not about facts — not about the evidence. The battle is about how you *interpret* evidence, which depends upon the history you believe to begin with. The real battle between Christianity and humanism, between creation and evolution, between Christian and non-Christian, is a battle between two different accounts of history — man's fallible view of history or God's infallible revelation of history. That's the real battle. We've got to recognize that the origins issue is really one concerning authority — God's Word versus man's word.

I was brought up in the secular education system and it's taken me years to try to "de-evolutionize" myself. But all of us are evolutionized in some way. People come to me and say, "Look, I'm trying to witness to a non-Christian and he says, 'Don't give me that Bible stuff, I don't believe the Bible. I want evidence; give me some evidence.'" When folks come to me with this dilemma, I say, *"Don't let them set the terms of the debate."* Again, the evidence is all the same. If you go out there and try to give them "evidence," what you're actually doing is giving them an interpretation of the evidence, and all they're going to do is reinterpret the facts. They are wearing a different set of glasses.

You need to set out to fit them with a new pair of glasses (biblical glasses) so that they will understand.

A girl came to me at a conference and said, "What you're saying makes sense. I go to Penn State University. We talk about ethics concerning using human embryos for research, and I have been telling my professors that it's wrong. However, I don't get anywhere with them." She paused, then continued, "I suddenly realized this morning that it's the glasses aspect I'm missing."

By and large, academics have a different foundation, a different set of glasses. We need to explain this to them by saying something like, "I can understand why you think the way you do. If you don't believe there's a God and you believe that we're a result of evolution, you're looking at the evidence and thinking, *What's wrong with using human embryos, we're just animals anyway*. But I want you to understand my position. I believe the Bible is the Word of

God; you might not, but I do. And because of that, I have a particular way of thinking. That's why I interpret the evidence the way I do."

Thus, you simply explain where your thinking is coming from. Also, consider Romans 10:17: "Faith cometh by hearing, and hearing by the word of God," and thus:

> How then shall they call on him in whom they have not believed? and how shall they believe in him of whom they have not heard? and how shall they hear without a preacher? And how shall they preach, except they be sent? as it is written, How beautiful are the feet of them that preach the gospel†of peace, and bring glad tidings of good things! (Rom. 10:14–15).

It's the Word of God that convicts, that is sharper than a two-edged sword. I'm not going to divorce my presuppositions from the way I interpret the evidence. Thus, I can say, "You might not believe the Bible; but I do. And what I want to show you is that, when I build my thinking on the Bible, I can make sense of the world. I can logically defend the Christian faith. I can show you that the statement "in the beginning, God created" fits with real science. I can show you that God created distinct kinds of animals and plants, and that this fits with what we observe in the world. I can show you that a global Flood makes sense of a worldwide fossil record. I tell them that I can't prove this explanation to them, because "without faith it's impossible"— but the more I argue this way, the more I'm showing that the Bible is the best explanation. I then go on to explain that they also need to listen to the rest of the Bible, including the Gospel.

Sadly, though, most Christian adults and young people don't think like this. Let me give you a simple (but often-overlooked) reason why so many believers fail to see the world through biblical glasses.

The Church has separated the Bible from the real world. They have been disconnected, if you will. As we'll see, the Church has accepted the world's teaching, and by doing so it has undermined the authority of the Word.

The statement of faith at most churches reads something like this: *The Bible is the ultimate authority in all matters of faith and practice.* Is there anything wrong with that statement? No, not in itself. I agree with the statement. But there is a problem with it that we're not seeing. Let's look at it this way: Where the Bible touches on geology, can we trust it? What about biology, astronomy, and chemistry?

Of course we can trust the Bible because it is the Word of God. The Bible is not just the ultimate authority in all matters of faith and practice. The Bible is the ultimate authority in all matters of faith and practice *and everything it touches upon* (which includes geology, biology, etc.). That's what I think the Church has missed.

In the 18th and 19th centuries, the idea that the earth is millions of years old became very popular. The bulk of the Church then basically said, "Okay, we can believe what the world is teaching about geology, biology, and so on, as long as the Bible is recognized as a book that teaches about morality and salvation." All of a sudden, the Bible was disconnected from the real world. The next short step was that the Bible no longer connects to death and suffering, the Grand Canyon, dinosaurs, and so on. That is why Christians end up asking questions such as, "How do you fit dinosaurs into the Bible?" They no longer understand that the Bible connects to the real world.

This thinking shows up in a big way in our Sunday school materials. In fact, I would say a lot of the Bible curricula that we use in the Church today, in many ways, totally miss the mark. Much of it is virtually worthless, because we have put the emphasis on cute animals and colorful packaging.

We teach Bible stories. Now what's wrong with that?

Isn't that what we're supposed to do? Shouldn't we teach the accounts of Jonah and the great fish, the feeding of the five thousand, Paul's missionary journeys, Noah and the ark, Adam and Eve? What's the problem with that?

Of course I believe all those accounts. The problem, however, is that people grow up looking on the Bible as just a collection of stories. From there it's a short leap to legend, myth, fairy tales. Not surprisingly, many denominations today teach that the Old Testament in particular was spun from myths and campfire stories. This inevitably leads to a weakening of the faith and outright assaults on the inspiration of the Bible, as seen in the antics of the Jesus Seminar "scholars" who tell us, among other things, that only 18 percent of the words attributed to Jesus actually came from His mouth.

We criticize television networks for inaccurate depictions of Bible figures, but that's exactly what we do in Sunday school and in our Bible curriculum. We teach our children Bible *stories*. Now here is what results from this short-sighted teaching method. These young people learn all these Bible stories, and then they go out into the big, "bad" world. Many end up in colleges and universities. They read magazines and books. But what they are taught in the world contradicts the Bible's history. Our young people are challenged by skeptics who ask questions that challenge the Bible's integrity. Questions such as:

- Where did Cain get his wife?
- Where did God come from?
- Where did Cain get his wife?
- How did Noah get all the animals on the ark?
- Where did Cain get his wife?
- Where did the races of people come from?
- What about the dinosaurs?
- How about carbon dating?

- Where did Cain get his wife?
- How about continental drift?
- Where did Cain get his wife?
- What about natural selection?
- Where did Cain get his wife?

So it goes. By the way, do you get the idea that Cain's wife is one of the most-asked questions? Interestingly, Clarence Darrow asked that question of William Jennings Bryan at the famous Scopes trial in 1925. Poor Bryan said that he didn't know.

> Darrow: Did you ever discover where Cain got his wife?
>
> Bryan: No, sir; I leave the agnostics to hunt for her.
>
> Darrow: You have never found out?
>
> Bryan: I have never tried to find out.
>
> Darrow: You have never tried to find out?
>
> Bryan: No.
>
> Darrow: The Bible says he got one, doesn't it? Were there other people on the earth at that time?
>
> Bryan: I cannot say.
>
> Darrow: You cannot say. Did that ever enter your consideration?
>
> Bryan: Never bothered me.
>
> Darrow: There were no others recorded, but Cain got a wife.
>
> Bryan: That is what the Bible says.
>
> Darrow: Where she came from you do not know?[1]

How can you preach the gospel to someone who asks the question about Cain's wife but doesn't get an answer? That question really challenges the Bible's history. If Christians can't explain how all people are descendants of Adam and Eve, why will people listen to any other teaching from the Bible? Theologically, if we're not all descendants of one man, Adam, then we have a major problem. Only descendants of Adam can be saved.

When an opponent of Christianity asks about Cain's wife, what he's really doing is challenging the historical accuracy of the Bible: "You believe this Bible? You believe this stuff? It says we start from Adam and Eve. Okay, you defend its history. Where did Cain get his wife?"

Most Christians give the same sort of answer that William Jennings Bryan gave. Your challenger then labels the Christian faith as a "pie-in-the-sky religion." He continues the assault: "You can talk about that morality stuff and salvation, but this has nothing to do with reality. The Bible is not history."

Sadly, most churches are not teaching adults or students how to connect the Bible to the real world. By and large they don't teach apologetics — how to defend the Christian faith and uphold the authority of the Word of God.

Consider this: in Sunday school — do we usually teach children about geology, biology, and astronomy? No? Why not? Well, in Sunday school we teach them about Jesus. If I can say this without being misunderstood, therein lies the major problem. The children end up thinking Sunday school and church is just about Jesus. Now this is important, but it comes across in most instances as just a "story."

You see, the Bible teaches about geology. It states that there was a global Flood. The Bible also teaches about biology. God made distinct kinds of animals and plants. The Bible deals with astronomy. God made the sun, moon, and stars on day 4 for signs and for seasons. Now the Bible doesn't deal with chemical equations or the laws of physics that helped put man on the moon, but the Bible *does* give the *big picture* in geology, biology, and other sciences, to enable people to have the right way of thinking about the universe. The Bible covers topics like the atmosphere and oceans. However we usually teach the Bible as just a collection of stories. Thus, children grow up thinking the Bible is just a book about morality and salvation, but what they learn in the world about geology, biology, and astronomy — that's what they can trust concerning the history of the universe. Eventually these students become consistent and say, "You know, if you can't trust the Bible's history, and you can't trust its geology, biology, and astronomy, why trust the morality and salvation?" And we lose these students to the world.

Hollywood actor Bruce Willis was interviewed for the *USA Weekend* magazine, and this is what he said regarding faith and morals:

> Organized religion used to hang the whole thing on one hook: if you don't do these things, if you don't act morally, you're going to burn in hell. Unfortunately, with what we know about science, anyone who thinks at all probably doesn't believe in fire and brimstone anymore. So organized religion has lost that voice to hold up their moral hand.[2]

Do you realize what he's saying? Here we are as a Church, claiming that abortion and homosexual behavior are wrong. However, the world is saying, "What are you talking about? Science has proved that the Bible can't be trusted anyway. And here you are holding up your morality based on that book. How can you say abortion and homosexual behavior are wrong, when we know this book can't even be trusted? Science has disproved the Bible's account of history."

Increasingly, the world views Christians as fanatics fighting moral issues, trying to impose Christian morality on the culture. However, most Christians don't realize that the culture no longer has a foundation that takes the Bible seriously. The Church itself, when it compromises with billions of years or evolution, has effectively said, "Well, we don't really believe the Bible's history." Then we wonder why we've got problems. We preach from a book that we admit can't be trusted in its history. We wonder why Christians are considered the "enemy," more and more, in this nation. And we wonder why Christians are considered to be bigoted, biased, intolerant people. Isn't that increasingly how we're viewed? The Church is trying to impose a morality on a culture that no longer accepts the foundation of that morality. And if we don't deal with that foundational problem, Christians will increasingly be seen as the enemy.

At the *Answers in Genesis* headquarters in Kentucky, we're going to build a creation museum. We had a four-year battle with the humanists over the right to use the property for a museum, but upon completion, visitors will walk in and learn how to put on biblical glasses. They will tour exhibits that illustrate the whole history of the world, through creation, corruption, the Flood, the Tower of Babel, Christ, the Cross, and consummation. They will see how the Bible connects to the real world, learning answers to the questions of the age. We'll teach the doctrines that are built on the Bible's history, and we'll proclaim the gospel of Jesus Christ. With a 2,000-foot frontage on a major interstate, we'll be shouting to the world, "The Bible is true! We can logically defend the Christian faith. You're going to be challenged to believe its message."

Let me give you another practical reason why a facility like this one is needed. Remember the blockbuster films *Jurassic Park* and *Lost World?*

You'll recall that *Tyrannosaurus rex* had teeth up to six inches long. Let me ask you a question. How would this dinosaur *originally* have been described? Was the creature a plant eater? A meat eater? Most people say it has always been a meat eater. Because we live in this present world and we observe animals with sharp teeth eating meat, we usually conclude that such creatures were always meat eaters. But if you put on your biblical glasses, you see things differently.

If you take Genesis as history, at face value, as written, Genesis 1:29 makes it very clear that God told Adam and Eve to eat fruit. He told the animals to eat plants. He did not tell the animals to eat other animals. In fact, this is substantiated in Genesis 9:3, where after the Flood, God told Noah he could now, for the first time, eat animals. That substantiates that Genesis 1:29 and 30 is teaching that man and animals were vegetarians — originally.

Now why am I emphasizing this? If you take Genesis to Revelation consistently, interpreting Scripture with Scripture, I believe you can come to no other conclusion than that death, bloodshed, disease, and suffering of man and animals are a consequence of sin. At the end of the sixth day of creation, God said everything was "very good." Would the world at that time be full of cancer? Do you think God would look on such disease and say, "That's very good"?

Now, if you believe in millions of years before Adam, you have no option but to accept diseases like cancer, death, bloodshed, violence, thorns, suffering, and extinction, as existing millions of years before man. There are some dinosaur bones in the fossil record (supposedly millions of years old) that show evidence of cancer. But the Bible's record makes it obvious such diseases are the result of Adam's sin. There are also *thorns* in the fossil record, supposedly hundreds of millions of years old, yet God specifically tells us that thorns are a result of the Curse. The stomachs of some animals were fossilized with the remains of other animals in them that they had eaten. If you believe in millions of years, you have to accept death, pain, killing, disease, thorns, struggle, suffering, and extinction before sin. How could God describe all that as very good?

Let us consider the death issue in more detail by looking more closely at the Book of Genesis.

How did Jesus interpret Genesis? In Matthew 19, when asked about divorce and marriage, He referred to Genesis as history:

> Have ye not read, that he which made them at the beginning made them male and female, And said, For this cause shall a man leave father and mother, and shall cleave to his wife: and they twain shall be one flesh? (Matt. 19:4–5).

What was Jesus teaching us? Do you want to understand the doctrine of marriage? The doctrine of marriage (and thus the meaning of marriage) is dependent upon its history being true. You become one. Why? It's based on the principle of "one flesh." Eve was taken out of Adam. If this event didn't happen in history, then how can you talk about oneness, as Jesus does in Matthew 19, and Paul in Ephesians 5? The woman couldn't have come from an ape-woman. To believe this is to destroy the whole basis of marriage. And we know it's to be a man and a woman and not a man and a man. Why? *Because God made a man and a woman in history, not a man and a man.* It grieves me, but does not surprise me, that the churches condoning homosexual behavior or ordaining homosexual pastors do not believe in a literal Genesis. If they did, they would realize that marriage could not be a man and a man, or a woman and a woman.

Ultimately, the history in Genesis 1–11 is foundational to every single biblical doctrine of theology. Why did Jesus die on the cross? Why do we wear clothes? Why is there sin? Why is there death? Why is Jesus called the last Adam? Why does man have dominion? Why is there a doctrine of work? Why marriage? Why a seven-day week? All these doctrines are founded in Genesis 1–11.

The history in Genesis 1–11 is foundational to the rest of the Bible. Incidentally, liberal teachers understand the best way to get rid of the Bible. First, get rid of the history (the geology and so on), because once the history's gone, it's then just some pie-in-the-sky religion, divorced from its foundation, and ultimately it will collapse. The Bible has been disconnected from the real world and relegated to just a collection of stories. No wonder people are leaving the Church. In the last 30 years, the United Methodist Church has lost three million members. Today, there are more Moslems in America than Episcopalians. The cause of this shift is no mystery!

The Church has been destroying its own history by believing in millions of years, taking man's interpretation of the evidence, adding it to the Bible. Discussions about Genesis and the whole issue of creation/evolution/millions of years, is an issue of authority. Do we take God at His Word or not? Is the Bible the infallible Word of God? And what right do we have to tell God what we think He means, instead of letting Him tell us what He said He did? That's the issue.

Another great controversy today concerning the Genesis history is the length of the creation week. If you don't believe that God created in six days, as His Word clearly states, then why believe Jesus Christ rose from the dead? Let me explain.

I'll tell you why I believe that Jesus Christ rose from the dead. Because the Bible clearly states that on the third day He rose from the dead. Some people claim we know Jesus rose from the dead because of all the evidence. However, all evidence is circumstantial. It's all interpreted. Even though the evidence seems to overwhelmingly support the claim that Jesus rose from the dead, ultimately, it is not proof. Ultimately, the proof is what the Word of God states. You know why I believe that God created in six days? Because the Word of God clearly states this. There is a beautiful quote from Charles Spurgeon, given during his last address to his pastor's college, in London:

Believe in the inspired volume up to the hilt.
Believe it right through; believe it thoroughly;
Believe it with the whole strength of your being . . .
The Scripture is the conclusion of the whole matter.

A call to battle for all of us, even today — especially today. You see, as soon as you question the six days of creation, you have lost the battle, and you may as well give up. Why? Let's look again at the Scopes trial.

Clarence Darrow persuaded William Jennings Bryan to get on the witness stand, because through Bryan (a dear Christian gentleman), he wanted to show the world that Christianity is a bankrupt religion. Darrow managed to get Bryan, representing Christianity, to be cross-examined concerning his faith, and it's interesting to read the transcript.

> Darrow: . . . .Does the statement, "The morning and the evening were the first day," and "The morning and the evening were the second day," mean anything to you?
>
> Bryan: I do not think it necessarily means a twenty-four-hour day.
>
> Darrow: You do not?
>
> Bryan: No.
>
> Darrow: Then when the Bible said, for instance, "and God called the firmament heaven. And the evening and morning were the second day," that does not necessarily mean twenty-four hours?
>
> Bryan: I do not think it necessarily does.
>
> Darrow: Do you think it does or does not?
>
> Bryan: I know a great many that think so.
>
> Darrow: What do you think?
>
> Bryan: I do not think it does.
>
> Darrow: You think those were not literal days?
>
> Bryan: I do not think they were twenty-four-hour days.

Darrow: Do you think those were literal days?

Bryan: My impression is they were periods, but I would not attempt to argue as against anybody who wanted to believe in literal days.

Darrow: Have you any idea of the length of the periods?

Bryan: No, I don't.

Darrow: And they had the evening and the morning before that time for three days or three periods. All right, that settles it. Now, if you call those periods, they may have been a very long time.

Bryan: They might have been.

Darrow: The creation might have been going on for a very long time?

Bryan: It might have continued for millions of years.[3]

Right then, the Christians lost the Scopes trial in the public mind. They lost the battle. Why? But didn't John Scopes get fined? Yes, even though it was overturned on a technicality. But I want you to think — that was 1925. Let's stand back and look at the big picture. Look at the culture. Is the culture today more pervaded by Christian influence or less than back in 1925? We would all agree it is much less Christian today. The Scopes trial was a turning point for Christendom in many ways. Christians lost the battle. Why? Because Clarence Darrow accomplished what he was seeking to do; he wanted the world to see, and the press to see, that when it came down to the bottom line, Christians really didn't believe what the Bible clearly said, and you can add millions of years to the Bible, thus reinterpreting the days of creation.

Today, there is great debate about the Genesis account of early earth history. Virtually any viewpoint is welcomed into the debating arena, except for the view that the Bible is plain in its language concerning the six literal days and thus a young earth.

However, I also have to say that I dislike the term "young-earth creationist." You see, when people use terms like "young-earth creationist" or "old-earth creationist," to me they're setting up a straw man in a way. To be frank, the priority is not whether you are a young-earth creationist. First and foremost, one needs to be a *biblical* creationist. For instance, the fact that I don't believe in billions of years is a consequence of biblical authority. It's not that I'm a young-earth creationist, and that's why I look at the Bible the way I do. It's because I look at the Bible the way I do that I cannot believe in billions of years, and thus I am a young-earth creationist.

Progressive creationist Hugh Ross says that those he labels "young-earth creationists" are putting a stumbling block in people's way, because they are telling people the world's not billions of years old when Ross says it is. Thus, Ross claims that if you let people believe in billions of years, that helps lead them to Christ, because it helps them to accept the Bible. But the opposite is true. For instance, the late Dr. Carl Sagan said this:

> If God is omnipotent or omniscient, why didn't He start the universe out in the first place so it would come out the way that he wants? Why is He constantly repairing and complaining? There is one thing the Bible makes clear, the biblical God is a sloppy manufacturer; He's not good at design, He's not good at execution, He'd be out of business if there was any competition.[4]

Notice what Sagan was saying. *Look at this world out there, all the mistakes, all the mutations, and the death and suffering and disease. Where's a God of love? Where is your powerful God? I don't see a powerful God.*

Now think about this question: Is this the world as

God made it? No. There is some beautiful design in our present world, but that misses the point. Kids are given a false idea in our churches — ah, look at the beautiful world God made.

Beautiful world God made? Go to Australia. It's a beautiful country, with the world's most poisonous sea snake, most poisonous snake, most poisonous jellyfish, most poisonous octopus, most poisonous stonefish, and man-eating crocodiles.

Irven Devore, from Harvard University, said this, "I personally cannot discern a shred of evidence for a benign, cosmic presence. I look at evolution; I see indifference and capriciousness. What kind of God works with a 99.9 percent extinction rate?"[5]

Irven Devore is looking at a fallen world. We know it was once perfect, but that is true only if you believe the history in Genesis. The world now is a broken one. But when a person believes that the world is billions of years old and that the fossil record is millions of years old, then such a person is really saying that the death and disease in this present world has been here for millions of years. Thus, God is to blame for all the death and suffering and disease. But the Bible doesn't blame God. Sinful humans are to blame. The death and disease are the result of our sin.

Now think about this. Here is where the rubber meets the road. If Adam's in your history, then God made you, God owns you, and God sets the rules. But if that history can be reinterpreted on the basis of man's ideas, then man is the authority. Who then sets the rules? You do. Why not reinterpret the Bible's morality? Why not reinterpret the Bible's salvation?

If the Bible's history is true, then the morality and salvation based on the Bible is true. However, if the geology, biology, and astronomy in the Bible can't be trusted, then why should one trust any of the Bible? The Christian who believes in millions of years reinterprets the geology in the Bible — then why shouldn't the rest of the Bible be reinterpreted on the basis of man's fallible ideas? Why not reinterpret marriage to allow for homosexual marriage, for instance?

However, when a Christian accepts that the Bible's history is true, then marriage is one man for one woman. One's world view is built on the Bible because the Bible's history is true. And when Adam's in your history, salvation is found in the "last Adam."

Unfortunately, our culture has replaced biblical history with a different history. When the Church has taught millions of years, then it has effectively taught that one doesn't have to believe the Bible's history. Thus, a door has been unlocked. Future generations push this door of compromise open even wider. They conclude that if the history in Genesis is not true, why believe the rest of the Bible? Why believe the morality and salvation? Why not write your own rules? Do what you want with sex. Abort babies — get rid of spare cats, get rid of spare kids, what's the difference? We see in our culture today the collapse of the Christian framework. We see an increase in the humanist philosophy. This is so because the foundation the culture was built upon has changed from one believing that God's Word is truth to believing that man's opinions determine truth. The foundation has changed from believing that God created in six days (thus, God's Word is true) to believing in millions of years (thus, man's word is true).

Friends, we need to contend for the faith. There is a spiritual battle in this world, and it's about time Christians were willing to stand up for what we believe, be bold, and deal with these issues. The creation movement is part of a movement that God has started to get people back to the foundation of His Word, beginning with Genesis.

In summary: The humanists are clever — how to try to get rid of Christianity? They know not to aim directly at the Resurrection or the virgin birth. They know to aim at the Bible's history of the world. Once the history's gone, the rest goes. And how have they done this? By convincing the Church to believe in millions of years and thus to reinterpret God's Word in Genesis. This unlocks the door to doubt in the authority of the Word, and this doubt spreads like a cancer through the culture and through subsequent generations.

Harvard, Yale, Princeton — how many of them were once Christian? All of them. How many of them are Christian today? None of them. Why? When you look into their history, they started to reject the truth in Genesis. They unlocked the door to further doubt in the Word of God. Subsequent generations pushed that door of doubt open to lead to the unbelief that we see today.

I have a challenge for you, and a plea to ensure that the Church stands on the Word of God from the very first verse. If we don't, the battle is lost. We might win little battles here and there, and we might see some successes with children. However, I wonder if in 75 years we would realize how even more devastating it had been for the Church to have allowed that door of compromise to stay open, by accepting millions of years — just as we look back at the devastation wrought by the Scopes trial, 75 years ago. Would we realize that we had a chance to restore the foundations of biblical authority, but we lost it?

While Christians take potshots at the "issues," the authority of Scripture is unraveling in people's minds. What do I mean?

We've spent millions of dollars fighting abortion. Guess what? It hasn't gone away. Why? Abortion is not so much the problem in itself; it's a horrific symptom of the problem. The real problem is the rejection of scriptural authority. This culture was once pervaded by a Christian influence, including prayer and Bible reading in the schools. The Ten Commandments were taught, and most children went to Sunday school and church. When the message of sin was preached in such a culture, people by and large understood. They could understand the message of Christ. They could even accept that things such as abortion and homosexual behavior were wrong — they were sin — even the non-Christians accepted that.

But we have new generations coming through an education system devoid of the knowledge of God. The Bible's history is ridiculed. Increasingly, people don't understand the Christian message. Neither do they accept the morality of the Bible. They have been brainwashed to believe that the Bible's history is wrong — so its morality and salvation are suspect, also.

What's the solution? The solution is we need to get out there and preach the authority of the Word of God without compromise. We need to show clearly that the Bible's history can be trusted. We need to give answers to the world's attacks on the Bible's history. The Church needs to tell the world that the millions-of-years theory is not true. The world needs to see Christians believing the Bible — not compromising with man's fallible words. As a result of this new vigor in the Church, we may see many saved and won to the Lord Jesus Christ. I think that too many people in American churches think that we need to go out there and change the culture. I disagree with them in one sense. I think we need to preach God's authoritative Word and proclaim that it is true history, so that people's lives and hearts and minds will be changed as they recognize their sin and their need of salvation.

Then *they'll* change the culture.

Endnotes

1 *The World's Most Famous Court Trial*, Bryan College, Dayton, Tennessee, 1990, p. 302.

2 *USA Weekend* magazine, *Cincinnati Enquirer*, Feb. 11–13, 2000, p. 7.

3 *The World's Most Famous Court Trial*, p. 302–303.

4   Carl Sagan, *Contact* (New York, NY: Simon & Schuster, Inc., Pocket Books, 1985), p. 285.

5   Irven DeVore, "Astronomy Might Be Refashioning Images of God," *Times-News Weekender*, May 1, 1999, Religion Section, p. 9A.

Chapter 3

THE FIRE BUILDERS

Jack Cuozzo

When I consider Thy heavens, the work of Thy fingers, The moon and the stars, which Thou hast ordained; What is man, that Thou dost take thought of him? And the son of man, that Thou dost care for him? (Ps. 8:3–4; NASB).

After contemplating the splendor of God's vast handiwork in the heavens and contrasting it to the seeming insignificance of mankind, David, "the sweet psalmist of Israel" (2 Sam. 23:1), penned these poetic words. From the depths of his soul, thoughts of praise and admiration arose from their dwelling place and magnified the Lord. Although he posed important questions of infinite value, it was neither the first nor the last time that these strong emotions beat within the heart of man.

At a much earlier date in history, Job, in a time of doleful uncertainty, rather than praiseful worship, burst out in the midst of his anguish and asked, "What is man that Thou dost magnify him, And that Thou art concerned about him?" (Job 7:17). Probing the mind of God, Job's

69

questions, almost identical to David's, emanated from pain rather than awe and wonder and cut deep into the fleshly problems of man's fallen condition.

Whether the question arises from a heart of praise or from a heart of sorrow, this inquiry has continued to echo through the canyons of time from generation to generation. In the course of its long and sometimes ponderous journey through the centuries, we find it inscribed in the New Testament letter to the Hebrews. In a moment of brilliant inspiration, it acquires a fresh new personality and sprouts forth like a bright green olive leaf. The pen of the writer to the Hebrews becomes more like an artist's brush and paints a picture of the Son of Man as if to illumine Old Testament eyes with a New Testament revelation.

In his inspired communication, the author of the letter to the Hebrews confirmed what was already known from the gospels, that the Son of Man of Psalm 8 is the Lord Jesus Christ, and that David had a dual and prophetic focus when he composed this sacred song: the love of God for mankind and the love of God for the Son of Man. It is in this major framework of God's concern for mankind that we are allowed to glimpse the love within the Holy Trinity and therefore the infinite presence of love in the entire breadth, length, height, and depth of the universe.

The question out of David's mouth can be examined in another way. For mankind to be included by the Psalmist in the same structure that declares the Father's love for the Son of Man is prophetic of John 3:16: "For God so loved the world, that He gave His only begotten Son." And why did God love the world? Psalm 8 provides that answer. David declared: "Yet Thou hast made him a little lower than the angels, and dost crown him with glory and majesty!"[1] (Ps. 8:5). The reason God loves man is because He created him. This fact remains true no matter how many clouds cover the mind of man.

This essence of God's eternal character is love, as John

wrote, "God is love, and the one who abides in love abides in God, and God abides in him" (1 John 4:16). There was love before there were any humans to love, before the world was created and before the beginning of time as we know it. This is communicated in Jesus' high priestly prayer: "For Thou didst love Me before the foundation of the world" (John 17:24).

A Spiritually Empty Universe

Therefore, we may confidently declare that love is the inherent environment from which we come, not a spiritually empty or impersonal universe. Conversely, if all men and women perceived their origins as accidentally arising out of a spiritually void universe merely composed of particles and space, the effect would be devastating. First, all love on earth would be foundationless, feigned, and superficial, and the basis for human relationships would go into extinction. The extinction of endangered species is alarming, but the extinction of love on earth would be fatal.

Try to imagine an impersonal universe, one without an omnipotent personal God. In your mind, travel backward in time, as far back as you can go in an impersonal universe. There's nothing out there but space, galactic matter, black holes, radiation, and so on. All you will ever find in this unproductive journey is matter and energy and, more importantly, it is silent on all the issues that confront mankind. There is no help out there for all the pressing needs of our day. Francis Schaeffer called this the "blank impersonal."[2]

Save Your Life or Lose It

Second, if in the midst of this perceived vacuum, men and women are taught that their true ancestors were primate animals that came down from trees and became adapted to walk, wouldn't that intensify their spiritual emptiness by reinforcing the presumed random nature of human existence? Because, if chance mutations, adaptations, etc. were responsible for transforming ape lower limbs ultimately into human legs for bipedal walking and upright posture, wouldn't it seem arrogant to think God made us upright from the beginning to be different from the apes? If chance mutations of australopithecine reproductive genes produced a bigger-brained *Homo* baby millions of years ago, would that constitute a meaningful beginning for the human race?

In direct contrast to New Testament instruction, evolutionary education stresses that our human roots are sunk deep in brutal warfare such as that between male apes fighting with each other over food, territory, and reproductive rights with female apes. This pseudo-evolutionary but true animal behavior contrasts with Jesus' words, "Do not be anxious then, saying, 'What shall we eat?' or 'What shall we drink?' or 'With what shall we clothe ourselves?' For all these things the Gentiles eagerly seek; for your heavenly father knows that you need all these things. But seek first His kingdom and His righteousness; and all these things shall be added to you" (Matt 6:31–33).

How foolish these words must sound to a cultural anthropologist professor who teaches courses about the necessity of fierce and deceptive behavior in early apes and hominids[3] for survival purposes.

Citing studies on the use of deception among primates to achieve success, evolutionist James Shreeve credited human intelligence to the use of deceit by our early ape ancestors. He wrote, "The sneaky skills of our primate cousins suggest that we may owe our great intelligence to an inherited need to deceive."[4] Would a God who used this Machiavellian method to increase our brain size also inspire Proverbs 24:28, ". . . And do not deceive with your lips"? And this is only a small part of the woes.

Once the Christian doors are opened for evolution to come slithering in and Darwin's followers become God's critics, is not the entire Bible held up to scrutiny under the magnifying glass of selectively advantageous versus selectively disadvantageous behavior? How selectively advantageous would loving your enemies and not "getting them back" be? How selectively advantageous were the actions of the early Christians in Rome who were thrown to the lions because they refused to worship Caesar? Would not a little feigned worship of Caesar have saved their lives and made good evolutionary sense? Yet, they did not consider their own lives more valuable than their relationship to Jesus Christ. This is so contrary to evolutionary standards that it defies the prevailing wisdom of this day as well as the pagan wisdom of Roman times. Paraphrasing the very un-evolutionary words of Jim Elliot, martyred missionary to the Auca Indians, "They are no fools who gave up something they couldn't keep for something they couldn't lose."

Therefore, the entire scientific idea of originating from a materialistic background, devoid of love and full of competitive anxieties, would obviously lead to increasing levels of individual selfishness. But we humans are already abundantly selfish due to our fallen nature. So, the natural result of this equation would not only be unsurpassed selfishness, but almost absolute certainty amongst intellectuals that our biblical origins were mythological. The distortions of our origins have had severe consequences.

How many Christians, in the midst of an evolutionary education, can abide in Jesus' famous words, "If anyone wishes to come after Me, let him deny himself, and take up his cross daily, and follow Me. For whoever wishes to save his life shall lose it"(Luke 9:23–24). The stark contrast is that evolutionary theory stresses "saving your life," at least until passing your genes on to the next generation. If Jesus is the author of evolution, why didn't He prescribe waiting to deny yourself until after you had procreated, and not before? What kind of physical survival strategy is that? In truth, it is the only kind for your soul to survive.

But I think Jesus meant it on both levels — a physical and spiritual denial of sinful practices.

But you say there was selfishness before Darwin. It isn't a new development. I agree and will go back even further in history to prove my point. There has been selfishness since the Garden of Eden rebellion. However, it is my opinion that this trait has never had the intellectual support it has enjoyed since the acceptance of Darwin's *The Origin of Species by Means of Natural Selection, or The Preservation of Favoured Races in the Struggle for Life,* "a book that sold out its first printing in one day and set in motion a controversy that has still not entirely subsided."[5]

What many people do not realize is that the modern scientific establishment, by fortifying the atheistic or agnostic world view with truckloads of evolutionary research to support the animal heritage and spiritually empty universe concepts, has justified the spiritual void within the heart and soul of man and simultaneously contradicted the words of Jesus Christ. Because of this reasoning, what the Christian community considers a state of "lostness," the public at large sees as a normal condition. Lostness due to sin and separation from a good God because of rebellion against Him is much different than lostness in an impersonal universe with a violent ape-human family history. In the first case, there is a solution — Jesus Christ; in the second, there is no escape from the predicament except to eat, drink, and take drugs, for "tomorrow we die." I believe that this second case is the reason for the increasing drug abuse in our generation.

The establishment of modern science stands in tremendous opposition to God at this place. I certainly am not condemning all modern scientists, but most of those who hold keys to the science kingdom at major universities and foundations are antagonistic to the biblical account of creation, and therefore are antagonistic to the very foundations of God's Word.

Douglas Futuyma of the State University of New York at Stony Brook gave us a good example of this attitude when he wrote, "By coupling undirected purposeless variation to the blind, uncaring process of natural selection, Darwin made theological or spiritual explanations of the life processes superfluous."[6]

That statement basically meant God was unnecessary and irrelevant in the explanation of the origin or maintenance of life, be it human or otherwise. Natural processes could account for everything. Phillip Johnson notes in *Darwin on Trial* how the National Academy of Sciences told the Supreme Court that the most basic characteristic of science is "reliance upon naturalistic explanations," as opposed to "supernatural means inaccessible to human understanding."[7]

Tim Berra of the department of zoology at Ohio State University carried it a step further in his book *Evolution and the Myth of Creationism.* He stated that creationists "are lobbying to have science classes teach the ideas of: a sudden creation from nothing by God; a worldwide flood; a young earth; and the separate ancestry of humans and apes."

He explained that these concepts came from the Bible and "are inherently religious." He then gave the reason why he believed they were "unscientific." It is "because they depend on supernatural intervention, not natural law."[8]

And this attitude has swept through the educational community at all levels, like a fire out of control. Sadly enough, there are Christians who have contributed fuel to this fire and could disparagingly be called "fire builders."

So, there you have it! For the public and most private school kids of America, the act of believing the biblical account of creation is "unscientific," and in this age when most children in our country either have their own computer or access to one, who wants to be unscientific or called unscientific by one's peers? It takes great courage by a youngster in school today to declare that he believes in a literal Adam and Eve in a science class. Or even worse, that Adam and Eve saw dinosaurs, when they supposedly died out 65 million years ago and, according to evolutionary calculations, men and women only evolved on earth somewhere around 200 thousand years ago.

Or, perhaps, courage of this sort may never be required at all, if the student comes from a Christian home or church that does not even discuss an original six-day creation or considers associating the perfect Son of God with ape-men in an imperfect world. Perhaps they have put things in the Bible that aren't even there to justify evolution. Still, the same problem remains that seems to have frightened so many Christians: How can a good God have used a vicious process to create man and never say one word about it in the Bible?

Sooner or later, this thought has to surface in a young mind because there's no way of getting around it. So, avoiding the question while he or she still lives at home just defers the problem to a later date when parents may not be able to influence them any longer. It is a question whose answer lies within the pages of the early chapters of Genesis, but most people don't feel competent enough to discuss it on a theological, let alone a scientific, basis.

After they move on to college, that son or daughter's faith begins to compete with the intellectual prowess of shrewd, sometimes atheistic professors who delight in destroying a student's literal understanding of Genesis. Could this be the reason that we are losing many of our children from evangelical and fundamentalist homes when they go to college, even Christian colleges?

Christian Friends Doubting the Validity of Genesis

Let's examine what my own son Joshua said in his junior year at the main campus of Penn State University in State College. Writing an article for ICR's *Acts and Facts*, Josh spoke about the reasons he and two friends at PSU started the "Origins Club." "Because," he said, "there was nowhere for students to turn when confronted with evolutionary ideas presented in class." He further elaborated on the urgency involved. "Many friends of mine who were actively involved in Christian organizations began to seriously doubt the validity of Genesis. Also those who did believe in creation had little or no facts to support its accuracy."

And so, very close to Valentine's Day in February of 1996, with Joshua Cuozzo as its president and Professor Stanley Mumma, Ph.D. as its faculty advisor, a loving scientific safety net called "Origins Club" had its first meeting for Christian students at Penn State who wanted to love God with all their heart, soul, and mind and give a reason for the faith and hope that was within them. It received the approval of the Undergraduate Student Government Supreme Court in April of 1996 and became an official organization on campus. It is still in existence at the time of this writing because capable faithful students have filled the positions of leadership since my son's graduation. More clubs like this are needed in other universities.

Origins Club was also a fishing net for the unsaved, as Joshua put it, "to reach out to the evolutionists and to encourage them to ask questions about what they believe and why. Christian or atheist, both agree that in order to promote good science there must be extensive educated debate and review. They should be willing to question their own theories as intricately as they question ours."[9]

Joshua's description of his Christian friends having doubts in the validity of Genesis strikes at the heart of us all. Who wouldn't have doubts when we are bombarded on every side by the so-called "facts" of science? Like these friends, many Christians are unwilling to make two categories in their mind for our origins: a scientific explanation and a religious explanation. This is a compromise position that turns Moses' account of creation into pure myth or allegory, and becomes, according to the Penn State students, invalid. Allow me to turn the tables on the evolutionists and illustrate with an analogy and an allegorical example.

An analogy: A foreign passport that has been forged and detected and declared "invalid" by U.S. customs agents at a border crossing will not enable that person to travel in the United States. It may even land him in jail. Likewise, a person with an invalid passport from Genesis cannot travel anywhere in the Bible without running into trouble. It is absolutely essential for sojourning and understanding in the land of the New Testament. Now the allegory.

Howie Discovers His Ancestors

Let's imagine that two Christians, Dave, a lab technician at a pharmaceutical company, and his boss, Howie, a former university professor, are going on a journey into the pages of the New Testament to visit the land of the early disciples of Jesus Christ. But in order to take this hypothetical trip they will need a valid passport from the Book of Genesis. They travel back to Genesis by merely opening pages, and when they arrive in Eden they purchase their passports. Although their salvation was free, they find that the Genesis passports are expensive, and Howie decides to shop around for a bargain. Dave purchases his from an angel at the normal price and Howie finally gets a bargain basement price from a snake. He even tries to chisel the snake down, but the snake is shrewd and won't be chiseled. The big sign in front of the snake's pit advertises "Down to Earth Deals." Howie worries a little about that, but the snake waves the passport in front of his face. Howie sees that its cover resembles a delicious, flattened dried fruit, is a pleasing pinkish color, and has "Genesis AA" stamped on its cover. The snake tells him that "AA" means "American Ancestry," and he is delighted to get an official document at such a bargain rate. He thinks his university friends will be impressed. Dave's passport is blue and has "Genesis AE" stamped on the cover, so Howie thinks it's invalid because the snake tells him it means "Artificial Event." He laughs at him for paying so much for an invalid passport all the way to the border of the New Testament.

They both arrive at the border crossing point into the New Testament and the customs agents tell them that Dave's passport is valid but Howie's is invalid! He is shocked and indignant and says that he paid perfectly good money to the snake. He says he thought "AA" stood for "American Ancestry." They reply that the snake lied. The agents say "AE" stands for "Adam and Eve" while his "AA" means "Ape Ancestry." They tell him to go back to Genesis and get an AE passport. Howie becomes very upset, and tells them the snake wasn't selling any AEs, he has no time or money (not true) to go back and buy another one, and what's wrong with an AA, anyway? He is now yelling at them incoherently and babbling on about how science has proved that apes were really our ancestors and that Christians shouldn't fight over non-essentials. However, Howie continues to fight over non-essentials with the customs agents and Dave, so they break up.

Dave crosses over at the checkpoint and goes on his way. Howie eventually sneaks in at a remote spot along the border in the middle of the night. Now, Howie is allowed to travel freely in New Testament Land, because he is obviously a saved Christian. It's only because he's carrying around an invalid passport that he will always have problems going back and forth between the Old and New Testaments. He may even be tempted to print AE next to his AA but that won't fool the authorities at the border, because they know that you can only have one or the other on the passport. Howie can't find Dave, so he decides to strike out on his own.

Other problems arise as Howie moves from town to town. After leaving Philippi he travels to Colossae, closer in the New Testament pages than they are in reality, and stays overnight. The next morning, when the shades of darkness are retreating and the first light of morning has dawned, after giving thanks for breakfast, he goes for a stroll downtown and spots a monument in the city square. On this block of granite are the words, "By Him all things were created" and "all things have been created by Him and for Him" (Col. 1:16). This makes him very uncomfortable, because somehow he can't quite understand how a sinless Son of God could use a sinful blood-stained evolutionary process as a mechanism to create men and women in a beautiful Garden of Eden that was called "very good." He remembers that the Master even referred back to Eden one day when asked about divorce between men and women of Israel. Jesus warned them, "Have you not read, that He who created them from the beginning made them male and female?" (Matt. 19:4).

The next day in Colossae, Howie decides to take a walk in the large park not too far from the inn where he is staying. He is just overflowing with gratitude for his faith in Jesus when he discovers another section of the letter from Paul that was on the monument. This time it is in a garden full of bright, colorful flowers. The fragrant scents permeate the air, and as he breathes deeply he is reminded of the original Garden of Eden where the air was so sweet with fruit blossoms and flowers, and the beauty so captivating that only true, 100 percent humans could appreciate, care for, and enjoy it. Trying not to think about being ripped off by the snake, he ponders how apes would completely trample this place, flatten the delicate flowers, and wreck the gardens. When he spots a sign in the midst of the gardenia bushes. He walks up to it and reads, "See to it that no one takes you captive through philosophy and empty deception, according to the tradition of men, according to the elementary principles of the world, rather than according to Christ" (Col. 2:8). Paul's thought clashes in his mind with the work of Jane Goodall, Dian Fossey, and Biruté Galdikas, who have studied non-human primates looking for clues to early man's behavior. Somehow, the elementary principles of the world that these women used in their work bore a close resemblance to those Paul told people to watch out for in his letter to the Christians in this town. Howie cannot picture ape-men and women in the Garden of Eden and wonders how Paul could have known about this.

He has been thoroughly confused now, because common sense, his own observations, and the verses from these letters that keep popping up in the most unusual places have almost convinced him to go back and get a proper passport. But Howie still has his reservations. However, back at the inn he picks up his copy of Darwin's *Descent of Man* published in 1871 and written by a man like him with the same frailties, insights, and hopes. He recalls that Darwin lost his faith during his scientific career, but Howie is thankful that he has kept his intact and blended it with evolution. Poor old Darwin, he just didn't know how to fit things together. On the way to his next stop in Thessalonica, Howie reads a section of his book to justify his ape ancestry position.

Once in Thessalonica he finds a local inn with a vacancy and after reading a few words by this learned man from England before retiring, he goes to bed from sheer exhaustion. As he drifts off to sleep he is wafted off into space and mystically transported into an old English country home. It is Charles Darwin's home in Down, England, and Howie recognizes the scientist seated at his desk. Somehow he is able to stand right next to him in his pajamas, without being seen, while Darwin is writing a letter. There's a strange, musty odor in the room so Howie holds his nose. Howie thinks this is a bit comical and tries very hard not to laugh, but there he is, standing in his pajamas, holding his nose next to the founding father of evolution. The irony is not lost on Howie. He looks down and sees "April 3, 1860" is written at the top of the sheet of stationary. He begins to read what Charles is writing. It is addressed to Asa Gray and while he is afraid of standing too close and being detected, he is able to observe this much: "I remember well the time when the thought of the eye made me cold all over, but I have got over this stage of the complaint, and now small, trifling particulars of structure often make me very uncomfortable. The sight of a feather in a peacock's tail, whenever I gaze at it, makes me sick!"[10] Darwin puts down his pen for a moment and lets the ink dry.

Howie is immediately whisked away back into his bedroom at Thessalonica and as he awakens he notices that the first rays of sunlight streaming through the slit between the window curtains are glinting off a crystal water pitcher on the washstand. What a pretty spectrum is scattered across the wall like a thousand tiny rainbows. Although these small trifling particulars of structure are physical, Howie is seeing them with his biological eyes, and the myriad radiance of their colorful glow makes him feel warm all over. They do not make him feel cold and uncomfortable, in fact, quite the opposite. They seem to grace the room with a spectacular and peaceful grandeur that makes him question Darwin's spiritual condition. Howie ponders that if Charles would have only asked the Lord to open his eyes, he could have seen nature's complexity in a new light and not been threatened by it.

He hurries down to breakfast because this is the last stop in his New Testament trip since he must check out this morning and return home. The waitress hurriedly throws a menu down in front of him and rushes off to see to another customer. He picks up the menu looking for scrambled eggs and reads the following:

Specials for Today:
Ostrich eggs done any way you like 'em.
Includes
Toast and coffee — 600 drachmas/ $2.00 American

Ostrich eggs! He's never even seen one, much less eaten one. He calls the waitress over to ask whether they have any of the old-fashioned chicken eggs and to inform her that he's not in the mood for anything so exotic as an ostrich egg. She explains to him that the boss got a special deal on these eggs because apparently ostriches just leave them all over the place and abandon them in the dust. Besides that, they don't have any chicken eggs today. He orders them, more out of frustration and hunger than desire, and glances down at the menu again. What's this?

"The ostriches' wings flap joyously With the pinion and plumage of love, For she abandons her eggs to the earth, And warms them in the dust, And she forgets that a foot may crush them, Or that a wild beast may trample them" (Job 39:13–15).

Immediately, a question comes to Howie's mind. What selective advantage is there in leaving eggs lying all over the place? If Darwin and the neo-Darwinians were right about survival of the reproductively fittest, an evolutionary numbers game, how did ostriches ever survive? That's pretty dumb; they should have all become extinct by now. His eggs arrive and somehow Howie just doesn't have an appetite left anymore, because in his scientific model, those eggs shouldn't even exist on his plate. He asks for the check, pays the waitress, and heads out the door. One last thing hits him while leaving, another sign by the cash register. He hates to look, but he does: "And for this reason we also constantly thank God that when you received from us the word of God's message, you accepted it not as the word of men, but for what it really is, the word of God, which also performs its work in you who believe" (1 Thess. 2:13).

That's it! Howie is convinced that he has the wrong passport. He decides to go back to Genesis to get a valid one with an AE stamped on the front. Howie finally realizes who his ancestors were and, besides that, he remembers an old Chinese proverb he once heard: "He who thinks he came from apes ends up with ostrich egg on face."

Thank you, dear reader, for allowing me to illustrate in an imaginative and amusing form, the terrible dilemma of a Christian who holds on to the irreconcilable dichotomy of creation and evolution in the Book of Genesis. Whenever confronted with facts such as our traveler encountered, there has to be an endless mental battle. This is part of the spiritual warfare that Paul described in the sixth chapter of his letter to the Ephesians.

And now, a further analysis of our present state of affairs.

Human Dignity

Over the course of approximately the last one hundred years, an enormous casualty has become evident. Because of the sickness and impending death of human love in our age due to the perceived spiritual vacuum and a plethora of presumed hominid fossils, human value has dropped to its lowest mark in centuries. Worse than the two famous stock market crashes in the past 70 years, the value of each individual human life has fallen like a stone. The enormous issue of human worth in general has raised questions that have left America gasping for answers. Human worth has been mortally wounded, and while people cry out tolerance, it is malevolence that has overcome our society. One of the most urgent problems at our present moment is the outbreak of school violence. A recent editorial cited a survey conducted in the Philadelphia area concerning this dilemma:

The most revealing comments came from the youngest writers. While adults have despaired, "How could Littleton happen?" teenagers aren't that surprised. They recognize that among their peers, in their schools, lack of respect is the norm.[11]

I have no doubt that lack of respect is the norm, but why is this true? Respect is the honor given to dignity, and dignity is born from the womb of human worth. Dignity is the quality or state of being worthy or esteemed, or feeling worthy or esteemed. Respect is the acknowledgment of that dignity and worth.

In a family (and we are all part of God's family), human worth is derived from being loved and valued as a person. Ultimately though, as discussed earlier, for worth to be enduring, it must originate from God's love. Familial love can bestow worth but it also can be lost quickly due to family breakdown. Too often the parties involved lose their sense of worth or dignity when love dies and respect quickly disappears thereafter.

It isn't accomplishments and winning medals and prizes that bestow a lasting dignity upon individuals, because sooner or later everyone loses at something, feels inadequate in some way, or becomes replaced by a younger, more capable person. No one can be successful all the time. Woe be to the athlete whose coach thinks he or she is only as good as their last game, race, or event. If fame and fortune brought lasting dignity, no famous person would ever commit suicide.

I do not have space or desire for many stories of famous people who have committed suicide, though a few examples will make my point clear. When you consider this grievous topic, you may immediately think of Ernest Hemingway and Marilyn Monroe. However, I'd like to take you back into ancient history, to one of the fathers of natural science and philosophy from Athens, Greece. Born in 384 B.C. in Macedonia, Aristotle was the founder of the Lyceum in Athens, a school devoted to the study of biology and the natural sciences. He was the boyhood tutor for Alexander the Great and in later life became embroiled in politics and rivalries. His "logic" became "the mould of medieval thought."[12] "Logic means, simply, the art and method of correct thinking. It is the *logy* of every science, of every discipline and every art."[13] Human paleontology, therefore, owes part of its name to Aristotle, so does anthropology, biology, physiology, cosmology, and so on. What happened to this great man of philosophy and science? Will Durant recalls the events that took place after he left Athens in exile in 322 B.C.

> Arrived at Chalcis, Aristotle fell ill; Diogenes Laertius tells us that the old philosopher, in utter disappointment with the turn of things against him, committed suicide by drinking hemlock. However induced, his illness proved fatal; and a few months after leaving Athens (322 B.C.) the lonely Aristotle died.[14]

This same kind of tragic story has been repeated over and over throughout the history of fallen man. So it therefore becomes of utmost importance and urgently expedient that we do not fail to recognize that which confers the greatest worth and dignity of all upon fallen man. This is the love of God, but the knowledge of its existence is on the wane.

We are losing faith in this magnificent love because over 125 years ago it began to be shredded by sharpened stone tools made by ancient man and later twisted by misconstructed and misinterpreted fossils of humans and animals. It was hidden in closed Paleolithic caves like Bernifal in France, where a dinosaur is carved on a wall in combat with a mammoth.[15] If that wasn't enough, this faith in God's love has been almost totally dissolved in the scientific test tubes of DNA labs by modern molecular biologists. In those laboratories, mixtures of chimpanzee genes and human genes have been teased and coaxed into demonstrating physical relationships that never actually existed at any time, in all of history. It has also been vaporized in dating laboratories used by archaeology and paleontology in techniques like thermoluminescence (TL), which attempts to determine the ages of sediments and burnt flints by heating them to high temperatures.

Faith in God's love has been buried with artifacts taken out of graves and subsequently filed away deep within museum cabinets, never to be shown to the public. It has been washed away by scrub brushes scouring redochre from Neanderthal remains so they would not reveal contemporaneity with more modern bones. It has been molded away by artificial plastic or plaster replacement of bone that is not faithful to the dimensions of the original specimen.

By each of these methods, faith in God's love is harmed, but by an even more insidious method, what I call the "paleontological gospel," there has been an attempt to substitute a parallel evolutionary faith for the biblical one.

The Paleontological Gospel

Once chemical and biological evolution is taken for granted, the unmistakable message from human paleontology is that many animals had to die so that men and women could live. Natural selection, which is the agent of death, not the angel of death, has been the scalpel blade that has carved mankind out of the rough substance of its animal predecessors. Presumably, many apes and hominids died so men and women could eventually have physical life as humans. Therefore, it is my belief that this parallel story, or paleontological gospel, has been offered to mankind to detract from the clear message of the Bible;

that is: Christ had to die so that men and women can live. He died and rose again so that we can have eternal spiritual life and at the pinnacle of our existence, eternal physical life in the resurrection.

However, if one tries to force evolution into the Book of Genesis, it must be grudgingly concluded that we received human life from apes and hominids and spiritual life from God. Apes and hominids died for us on one hand and Christ died for us on the other. Therefore, we have the gospel according to human paleontologists and the gospel according to God. And they say evolution is not a religion.

Besides the obvious blasphemy, there are many problems with this story. First: Why would God love the children of more-advanced apes (us) more than the children of the smaller-brained apes that now reside in zoos, rainforests, etc.? Were the former made in His image while the latter were not? As you peer down the deep dark corridors of the presumed evolutionary history of *Homo sapiens,* please note carefully when you begin to spot this gift of image of Godness shining through one of these extinct apes. Search through all the magazines, textbooks, and scientific articles that you care to and try to determine where this event occurs in hominid history. In other words, try and find Adam and Eve among the ape-like creatures that existed before man in the pages of *National Geographic* or similar publications. I think you will be disappointed.

For the sake of argument, perhaps you may say it was when these ape-like animals started being creative and making stone tools that they became human. "See!" you say, "God's creative; so are these creatures!" By George, you think you've got it! That's where the image of God enters evolutionary history. Yes, but chimpanzees also use tools. Chimpanzee researchers in Taï National Park, a 1600-square-mile tropical rainforest in the Republic of the Ivory Coast found:

To extract the four kernels from inside a panda nut, a chimp must use a hammer with extreme precision. Time and time again, we have been impressed to see a chimpanzee raise a twenty-pound stone above its head, strike a nut with ten or more powerful blows, and then, using the same hammer, switch to delicate little taps from a height of only four inches. To finish the job, the chimps often break off a small piece of twig and use it to extract the last tiny fragments of kernel from the shell.[16]

Therefore, looking for stone tool use in early hominids as a way of looking for Adam and Eve becomes a "shell game."

To make matters more complex, every single one of those early animals or ape-humans had a mother. According to Genesis, Adam and Eve were made in the image of God and had no mother. I have never heard of any paleoanthropologist suggesting that from the time the human and chimp lineages allegedly split five million years ago, there was an innovative reproductive event. If there was, it might have gone something like this: "Suddenly out of the body of a male *Homo erectus* popped a fully grown, oh my goodness, female *Homo erectus!* 'Ou, La, La!' said the male to the female. 'Dabba, dabba dabba,' said the female to the male. All day long they babbled away, in a *Homo erectus* kind of way." And now back to reality.

According to all reports the last time I visited a zoo, chimpanzee mothers were still giving birth to little chimp babies. Therefore, if there were such things as hominid mothers, they would give birth to baby hominids. That's just the way the world works. It's not too complex to understand. Therefore, if you are a Christian and you'd like to fit evolution somewhere in the Bible, when you look for

Adam and Eve in the fossil record make sure that neither of them had mothers.

Man Is Special

There was no man who knew more about mankind than Jesus Christ, who was fully God and fully man. He knew that man was very important because as Paul wrote: "by Him all things were created," both "by Him and for Him."(Col. 1:16). So, in His own words in the Sermon on the Mount, Jesus reaffirmed the high value of mankind by comparing us to some of His other creatures. "Look at the birds of the air, that they do not sow, neither do they reap, nor gather into barns, and yet your heavenly Father feeds them. Are you not worth much more than they?" (Matt 6:26).

What did Jesus say here? Did He really say humans are worth more than birds? This may seem very reasonable to those who believe God's Word, but it wasn't to Napoleon Bonaparte. Trinkaus and Shipman reported that Napoleon Bonaparte appointed 12 professors to newly created posts between 1793–95 in the new Museum of Natural History in Paris. Four of those posts were concerned with fossil research and related issues. Why did the "soon-to-be-emperor" do this?[17] The answer may be found in Napoleon's conversation in exile at St. Helena while discussing his beliefs in man's origin and his relationship to the animals:

> Say what you like, everything is matter, more or less organized. When out hunting I had the deer cut open, and saw that their interior was the same as that of man. When I see that a pig has a stomach like mine, and digests like me, I say to myself, "If I have a soul, so has he." A man is only a more perfect being than a dog or a tree, and living better. The plant is the first link in a chain of which man is the last. I know

that this is all contrary to religion, but it is my opinion that we are all matter."[18]

For those Christians who think like Napoleon and try to squeeze some sort of natural progression of creatures into their religion, it presents a further dilemma. Why were humans worth more than the so-called "feathered dinosaurs"? Were humans worth more because they had climbed to a higher level as Napoleon had crudely imagined? And did God confer an eternal soul on them because they had won the evolution numbers game? From a biblical perspective, this would become a pride issue and we know what the entire Bible has to say about human pride. Proverbs 16:18 states it clearly, "Pride goes before destruction."

But viewed from a purely evolutionary perspective, it presents a different set of problems. Belief in value judgments based on higher or lower positions on the tree or bush of life is now a politically incorrect view.

Animals Are Special, Too!

Jesus' Sermon on the Mount statement about our value in contrast to the birds does not sit well with modern evolutionists like Donald Johanson, the discoverer of "Lucy." He and Blake Edgar wrote "to a large extent, creation myths glorify the specialness of humans."[19]

For Jesus to make a statement that emphasized the specialness of humans would seem to indicate, even to a casual observer, His reinforcement of "a creation myth" as defined by Johanson and Edgar. Are Christians who believe in evolution unwittingly accepting this fraudulent analysis of our Lord's own words?

The radical conservationists and the animal rights activists also do not agree with Jesus' definition of human versus animal worth. But before I begin on this subject, it is important to state that all Christians should be environmentalists. Taking care of the earth that God created is essential because first, it was a commandment to Adam;

second, it makes common sense because the opposite extreme of air and water contamination is destructive of nature and human and animal lives. I saw some river pollution in East Germany when I was there in 1991 and it was awful. That's not what I'm discussing here.

What I do maintain is that animal-activism taken to an extreme, borders on insanity. There should be a careful balance on these issues. For instance, in 1978 the lives of an endangered species of fish, the three-inch snail darter of the Little Tennessee River, were protected by a United States Supreme Court decision, which held up the filling of the $116 million Tellico Dam with water because of its potential harm to these tiny creatures.[20] However, at that same moment in time, because of a Supreme Court decision in 1973, the lives of unborn *Homo sapiens sapiens* babies were being destroyed at the rate of one million per year in medical settings supposedly dedicated to the preservation of human life.[21] Schaeffer and Koop cite a $340 million dam on the Stanislaus River in California that "ran into legal difficulties because a 5/8-inch daddy-long-legs spider dwells there."[22]

A group called the Animal Liberation Front has recently been engaged in violent behavior that has prompted the U.S. Senate to toughen penalties for these crimes. A report in the June 3, 1999, *Nature* magazine details the latest outbreak of vehemence by these animal rights activists. "When a dozen laboratories at the University of Minnesota's Twin Cities campus were attacked in early April, word of some $2 million worth of damage and 116 lost animals spread quickly in the scientific community."[23] Meanwhile, humanist scientists are gearing up for human cloning.

This is horrendous, but probably a natural consequence of the evolutionary philosophy that has elevated the value of animal life beyond that of man. If you think me wrong at this point, listen to what Andreas Kreiter, head of the University of Bremen (Germany) Research Center for Cognitive Neuroscience, said in an interview for the June 1999 issue of *Science* magazine.

> In Germany it now seems to be easier to get permission for [an experimental] study involving humans than it is to get permission for animal experiments. The trend frightens me. I see a tendency to try to balance out animals against humans.

Kreiter conducts his research in a facility that looks more like a "top-secret weapons lab than a university research institute." The building has a chain-link fence topped with razor wire surrounding it. "A three-meter-wide poster set up in downtown Bremen in 1997 branded him a 'monkey torturer' and listed his home and lab address." He has received death threats and "armed police escort him when he makes public appearances."[24] Denis Duboule, a developmental biologist at the University of Geneva in Switzerland had a warning spray-painted on his home because he used mice in his research.[25]

Why are medical researchers' lives threatened so viciously in our generation? An obituary for a Tanzanian chimpanzee named Flo that appeared in the *London Sunday Times* may give us a clue. It was written by Jane Goodall about her dead chimpanzee friend Flo who died a natural death in the Gombe Reserve. (As far as I can tell, Flo didn't have a last name.)

> Flo has contributed much to science. She and her large family have provided a wealth of information about chimpanzee behaviours — infant development, family relationships, aggression, dominance, sex. . . . But this should not be the final word. It is true that her life was worthwhile because it enriched human understanding.

But even if no one had studied the chimpanzees at Gombe, Flo's life, rich and full of vigor and love, would still have had a meaning and a significance in the pattern of things.[26]

To put this into proper perspective I quote from my book, *Buried Alive*:

> This does not imply for one moment that man should mistreat nature or animals and that the Bible has ever given him the license to do so. In fact, it is quite the opposite. The Bible says, "A righteous man has regard for the life of his beast" (Prov. 12:10). Nature should be placed in its proper order. It means God is to be worshiped and nature cared for, not the other way around as you hear from the liberal pulpit. Nature is not to be worshiped.[27]

Now, of course, I am certainly not blaming Jane Goodall for the entire animal activist movement. This is only one example of the kind of thinking that has resulted from the whole evolutionary movement of the last century or so.

Biruté Galdikas was interviewed about her 15-year involvement with orangutans in the rainforests of Borneo. Confronted with the question about her first husband Rod's leaving her, she replied, "Rod left saying I loved orangutans more than him."

But, in an attempt to protect her image, she contrasted herself with the famous gorilla expert, the late Dian Fossey:

> There is an important way that Dian and I are different. I think she was stuck in a place where she believed gorillas were better than humans. They're not. They do all sorts of terrible things, like kill each other; though perhaps they do it without malice, unlike us. Dian died be-

lieving the worst about people. Maybe in that sense she was committing suicide.[28]

Although she denied having Fossey's attitude about humans, she commented about her orangutans' loner-type behavior:

They've gone off on a path divergent from ours and developed this incredible strength of character denied us because we are a gregarious species.

Therefore, I conclude from this is that she is implying that humans do not have the strength of character of orangutans. With statements like this, you shouldn't wonder why our children are confused about who is made in God's image and who isn't.

The most recent attempt to grant chimps a closer-to-human status has come from a combined research effort in Africa published in June of 1999. With results from seven long-term studies, altogether representing 151 years of chimpanzee observation, Andrew Whiten, Jane Goodall, and seven others concluded that chimps invent and socially communicate new techniques and customs that should be designated as cultural achievement. They cited 39 chimp behavior patterns, including five nut-hammer variations.[29] Frans B. M. de Waal who is at Living Links, the Yerkes Regional Primate Center and Department of Psychology, Emory University, Atlanta, Georgia, commenting on these 151 combined years of chimp study wrote, "Biologically speaking, humans have never been alone — now the same can be said of culture."[30]

What Dr. Frans de Waal and Napoleon had in common would be a good trivia question. However, the matter is anything but trivial. Personally, I believe cultural anthropologists have wasted an enormous amount of time and resources trying to document our supposedly close relationship to the chimpanzees. But I will retract that statement if a chimp ever writes an article or a book to refute my position.

Therefore, my understanding of why animal-activist violence is a natural outgrowth of evolutionary thinking focuses on a central theme: medical researchers are preventing the animals, not just primates, even mice and rats, from enjoying rich and full lives with vigor and love, which also have meaning and significance. It is almost like an animal Declaration of Independence: life, liberty, and the pursuit of happiness. There is one big difference. Animals didn't write it, humans did. In accordance with my line of thought above, when animals compose their own Declaration of Independence we can begin taking evolution seriously and mice – besides Mickey – can enjoy meaning and significance. The main point being, do we treat animals' lives reasonably as the Bible advocates or do we put them on a pedestal?

Animal Humor Rooted in Creation

In the meantime, we can continue to laugh at typical American humor in the form of comics in the Sunday papers – old Bugs Bunny cartoons and the like. But, how funny would Daffy Duck be if he didn't act human? What about Sylvester the Cat, Tweety Bird, and all the Far Side characters? Why do they strike humans as funny? Even the die-hard evolutionists find them amusing. While doing some research at Harvard's Peabody Museum, I saw a Far Side cartoon in the hallway of the Human Paleontology area. Why do humans find animal humor funny? I think it is because we know down deep, no matter who we are, unless our ability to understand is clouded by mental illness or deficiency, that animals are just animals, but we are very different, very special. The fact that humans are made in the image of God, whether we realize it or not, rises to the surface whenever they see the coyote chasing the road runner who goes "beep-beep" or cows standing on two legs talking to each other in a pasture.

Thus, it is because of how we were made that this sort of humor is funny even to children. If there was nothing inside of us that made us aware of our huge difference, we wouldn't laugh. So, it seems to me that God's creation of individual kinds, especially the creation of man and woman separate from the animals, is the basis of all animal humor, or for that matter vegetable humor (vegetables acting like people). The good thing about this kind of humor is that it reinforces an awareness of the image of God inside of humans. This prime factor must be responsible for the enduring value of this form of humor in our culture. Now you know why people like Snoopy birthday cards.

In contrast, the modern type of space-alien cartoon does not highlight this animal-human difference, so it must work hand-in-hand with evolutionary influences that equate humans and animals. Awake America! Which kind do you think children ought to be reading and watching?

Human Paleontology's Profanity

In our sophisticated scientific day there has been a deliberate omission by paleoanthropologists. Anthropology is the study of man, while paleoanthropologists study ancient "fossil" man and all of the supposed hominid ancestors. As discussed earlier, questions concerning man's origin and nature have been around for a long time and will continue to be. Little children want to know where they came from, and adults search for their true identity. All of us have thought about these questions at one time or another. Science also asks these questions, but now they are purely rhetorical because modern science no longer considers God to be the Father of mankind. It already knows the answers and merely seeks after naturalistic processes as explanations to satisfy the longings of man's mind. These answers will never satisfy the longing of man's heart because the questions are addressed only to colleagues in the profession and not to God.

In the grievous lament of Job, the awestruck wonder of David, or the fresh and vital message of the author of Hebrews, there was always this common denominator: the questions were addressed to their Heavenly Father. This is no longer true. The modern version is now just, "What is man?" Modern biologists and anthropologists ask each other this question. They go back and forth in competition, shooting down each other's naturalistic theories and for that reason call science "self-correcting." Their answers are always based on materialistic research which actually needs a little God-correcting rather than self-correcting. Today, man is matter in motion, just a fire builder who became a rocket builder, another animal and a product of DNA and RNA.

In their book *Origins*, Richard Leakey and Roger Lewin provide a good example of the typical modern form of the eternal question:

> There appears to be a universal curiosity about our past, about how a thinking, feeling, cultural being emerged from primitive ape-like stock. What evolutionary circumstances molded that ancient ape into a tall, upright, highly intelligent creature who, through technology and determination, has come to dominate the world? This is the question we ask about ourselves.

This is not all. They continue with the thoughts — or should I say doubts — behind this question.

> And it is not mere idle curiosity because without doubt, the key to our future lies in a true understanding of what sort of animal we are.[31]

Notice what they said about the circumstances that molded man: they were "evolutionary" not supernatural. Are there God-breathed genes running through your veins or re-hashed ape genes? The choice is up to you and its importance cannot be overstated. I cannot say it strongly enough nor emphasize it convincingly enough, but the choice you make will affect the dignity of men, women, and children until the Lord returns.

Allow me to help you make an informed choice based on historical facts. Our future does lie in a true understanding of who we are, whether it be an animal heritage as Leakey, Lewin, and scores of others allege or a godly heritage as David, Job, and the writer to the Hebrews maintain. What do you think?

Anthropology's Position

The first fossil to throw the world in a tizzy was the famous Neanderthal adult male discovered in 1856 in a cave, in a valley ("thal") in Germany, named after the hymn writer Joachim Neander. This name stuck, and from then on all fossils with similar features were called Neanderthals or Neandertals.[32] Although it was not a complete skeleton, a partial skull and enough bones were discovered to show the world that people looked different in an earlier time. Was it diseased, ape-like, or something else?

These ancient remains and others like them have been the cause of much midnight oil being burned by many researchers including "yours truly." Having spent many hours in museums in Europe and the Middle East, I have found some startling scientific facts about these remains. I have studied, photographed, and x-rayed the actual bones of Neanderthal men, women, and children. My conclusion is that the world has not been told the truth about Neanderthal man. I cannot say that emphatically enough. For all my critics, let me say I did not take religious x-rays. The x-rays I took are the same kind that orthodontists use around the world. Too often we have had to accept the research of evolutionary paleoanthropologists as the final word on the subject. Well, now we don't have to anymore.

We have had to swallow statements like the following for too long. It comes from Eric Trinkaus and Pat Shipman in their book *The Neandertals* concerning the man from the Neander Valley.

> The new man, in his glowering silence and mystery, would show Fuhlrott and others — however much they squirmed and argued — the unthinkable: that humans were animals too.[33]

I have demonstrated in my book *Buried Alive* that this is an incorrect conclusion. I must refer you to this extensive study so that you may be convinced that there is real scientific data behind the position that adult Neanderthals were very old people, but not exactly like us.[34] They were closer to Adam and Eve in time and genetics, and since the Fall had progressive consequences for humans, obviously they would not be exactly like us. At present we are in a degenerative condition compared to Adam and Eve, the pre-Flood and early post-Flood peoples. We are unable to exist to the old ages that were attained by the patriarchs.

There is no one in recent history who has lived to 600 years like Shem, 464 years like Eber, or even 180 years like Isaac. Our average life expectancy is 75 years, and maximum longevity about 115 or 120 years.[35] I have given scientific evidence demonstrating that Neanderthals lived in the range of 250 to 300 years of age, perhaps more. I believe this should stimulate more research along these lines so we can view man correctly: created perfectly and subsequently fallen in spiritual and physical nature. It is my hope that this contribution to Christian Human Paleontology will spark a fire under other workers to move ahead in this area. Let's look again at some of the distortions of the past that have put us in this situation.

Charles Darwin's *Origin of Species* was published in 1859, and in that same year Paul Broca founded the Society of Anthropology in Paris, France.[36] Eleven years later, Broca boldly set the tone for future study in this subject when he declared in 1870:

> As for me . . . I would much rather be a perfected ape than a degraded Adam. Yes, if it is shown to me that my humble ancestors were quadrupedal animals, arboreal herbivores, brothers or cousins of those who were also the ancestors of monkeys and apes, far from blushing in shame for my species because of its genealogy and parentage, I will be proud of all that evolution has accomplished, of the continuous improvement which takes us up to the highest order, of the successive triumphs that have made us superior to all of the other species . . . the splendid work of progress.[37]

This proclamation by the founder of an infant discipline of science had two distinguishing marks. The first was its obvious loathing of his true biblical heritage accompanied by his desire to shed its implications. The second feature was an expression of hope and faith in a new method of escape from the human predicament by means of human evolution. The human predicament is sin and all its effects. Degraded Adams and degraded Eves need Jesus Christ. This apparently was unacceptable to Broca.

A Prehistoric Gettysburg?

Did anyone ever tell Broca that if evolution really did take place, the kind where apes were transformed into people, called macroevolution, there had to be dead animal and ape-man remains in the ground when the Lord declared it all to be "very good" on the sixth day (Gen. 1:31).

Even if there was an alleged huge gap in history between the first two verses in Genesis, and the fossils were deposited at that time, the ground had to be full of human and animal bones and blood on the sixth day. So when the Lord re-created (according to some Christians), the soil was not pure by any means. It contained a history of death. Adam and Eve, at the end of six days or 4.5 billion years, had to be standing on ground that was more hallowed than the Civil War battlefield at Gettysburg. If this fact were true, even Abraham Lincoln could not do justice to all that lay slain in the earth from the evolutionary wars.

But God built no memorial monuments, laid no wreaths, nor did the angels play heavenly "taps" on their trumpets. Instead, He declared it all "very good." This was not a Memorial Day speech in honor of the dead; it was the proclamation of "the beginning" and not a new beginning.

If the earth was not void of dead remains, how might Cain have replied to the Lord when He said to him, "What have you done? The voice of your brother's blood is crying to Me from the ground." If the ground of the earth resembled a prehistoric Gettysburg, might not Cain have been justified in irreverently replying to God like this: "There has been blood in the ground for millions of years, Lord. What is so special about my brother's blood? My grandfather's blood and bones lie in a cave over yonder. He was slashed in the neck by a saber-toothed tiger while he was sleeping. I heard from my father Adam that his uncle to the fourth power strangled his *Homo erectus* wife out of jealousy because she fell in love with a Neanderthal man. Besides all that, australopithecines have been killing each other for millions of years!" And with the height of irreverence and disrespect he might have capped it off with "And You called all of that bloody ground very good on the sixth day! What's so bad about my brother's blood in the ground? Why is it not so good now?" Irreverent as it would have been, he would have had a good point. But this was not the case. Cain could not say anything like that, because Cain had no grandparents and Adam, no uncles. There were no fossils in Eden. It's about time Christians wake up and see the truth.

Devolution

One of the reasons paleoanthropologists have concentrated all their efforts into showing a progression of apes to men is because men and apes are devolving downward, not evolving upward. Now, I realize that paleoanthropologists don't like the use of "up" and "down" anymore, but when the human race is degenerating, I don't know what else to call it. In *Buried Alive,* I use numerous examples from recent science and ancient history to document that fact. I think the evolutionists fear devolutionary evidence and that has been the reason behind many of their misconstructions.

Regardless of what evolutionists think about the Lord, they're all going to meet Him one day. No human being will escape his date with eternity and the Almighty. It is my belief that no Neanderthal escaped this date. How can I say this with confidence? According to our calculations, the remains of ancient human beings that lived in the vicinity of 200 years of age look like Neanderthals. Even Abraham at 175 years probably appeared somewhat Neanderthalish. Let me state again, because it is obvious that they were closer to Adam and Eve than we are, and the effects of the Fall are progressive, they had to possess greater genetic strength. We have lost that strength and consequently die sooner. We have devolved, not evolved.

Neanderthals in the Resurrection

Now that you understand who Neanderthals were, we can move on and discuss their place in eternity. In the Old Testament we find David has written, "For thou wilt not abandon my soul to Sheol" (Ps. 16:10). Even earlier in history Job had said in the midst of his torment and suffering, "And as for me, I know that my Redeemer lives, And at the last He will take His stand on the earth, Even after my skin is destroyed, Yet from my flesh I shall see God" (Job 19:25–26). It is therefore without a doubt that these two men, David and the venerable Job, fully expected God to save their immortal souls and thereby experience His presence.

But where did the souls of men and women of faith go after death before Jesus Christ was resurrected from the dead? The answer is given in the Scripture where Jesus told of the rich man and a poor man named Lazarus who both had died and went to two very different places. Lazarus was carried by angels to the extremely pleasant Abraham's bosom which was far away from Hades, the rich man's flaming repository. In anguish and pain the no-longer-rich man yelled out for Father Abraham to have mercy on him. However, it was too late for that and his agony continued because he couldn't cross over the enormous fixed chasm between the eternities (Luke 16:19–31). Very high stakes we're talking about here! Life is no game that we can play again next season!

A special position belonging to two men of faith is also revealed in the appearance of Moses and Elijah in their glorified bodies in front of a startled Peter, James, and John at the transfiguration of Jesus (Luke 9:28–36). In my opinion, this occurrence was a preview of how a glorified body will appear to people who still have their "earthly bodies," as Paul would call them.

Paul expressed consternation at people who would ask, "How are the dead raised? And with what kind of body do they come?" (1 Cor. 15:35). He replied to this question by saying, "You fool!" And after emphasizing the differences between the bodies of physical creatures he proceeded to explain the differences between the natural human perishable bodies and those that they would gain at the resurrection which would be "raised an imperishable body" (1 Cor. 15:42).

Jesus gave us another glimpse into eternal life in heaven when He replied to the questions of the Sadducees who didn't believe in a resurrection of the dead. He said:

> For when they rise from the dead, they neither marry, nor are given in marriage, but are like angels in heaven. But regarding the fact that the dead rise again, have you not read in the book of Moses, in the passage about the burning bush, how God spoke to him, saying, "I am the God of Abraham, and the God of Isaac, and the God of Jacob? He is not God of the dead, but of the living; you are greatly mistaken"(Mark 12:25–27).

This then is the final authority on heaven and on earth informing us that there are living souls in heaven with Him and that there will be a bodily resurrection for those declared righteous by God.

Neanderthal Faith Reckoned as Righteousness

Concerning Abraham, we read in the Book of Genesis, "Then he believed in the Lord; and He reckoned it to him as righteousness" (Gen 15:6). Paul also emphasizes Abraham's life-saving faith in chapter 4 of his letter to the Romans. We also know that Abraham was 175 years old when he died and his soul departed from his perishable body (Gen. 25:7–8).

I know from my research in paleoanthropolgy that Abraham must have begun to look like a Neanderthal at that age. Certainly not as much like a Neanderthal as Shem who died at age 600 or Noah who died at 950 years. I do not know about the faith of Shem but I can comment on the faith of Noah because God said to Him, "For you alone I have seen to be righteous before Me in this time" (Gen. 7:1).

Therefore, we can be sure that at least one person (Noah) who had all the aged features of a Neanderthal in his perishable body will have an imperishable one that we may not recognize. We *can* be sure he will be resurrected from the dead.

As for the righteousness of any other ancient men and women, we can only speak when God has spoken. All I can say with confidence is that Neanderthal features are not an impediment to being declared righteous before God, because these features are purely the physical characteristics of ancient people. In their younger ages (as you know if you have read *Buried Alive*), their physical appearance was unique but closer to ours, and as they surpassed us in age because of their superior genome, they became what we know today as adult Neanderthals. My guess is that there are probably many of them in heaven. Will we recognize them? I don't know. John tells us in his first letter, "Beloved, now we are children of God, and it has not appeared as yet what we shall be. We know that, when He appears, we shall be like Him, because we shall see Him just as He is" (1 John 3:2).

We don't know yet what we will look like so we cannot know how they will appear. But they were people who had souls. There is obviously no one with any biblical knowledge who would debate whether Noah was a real human with a real soul and was righteous. To the best of my knowledge after 20 years of scientific study, I know from my work that Noah's features should resemble those of a Neanderthal, since he lived to 950 years. If we lived that long we would surely resemble a Neanderthal, also. Consequently the debate about Neanderthal souls should be over. They had them. They will be there. My hope and prayer is that you will be, too.

Endnotes

1 That word "angels" is translated from the Greek in the letter to the Hebrews. In Psalm 8 it is the Hebrew word for God, *Elohim*. However I utilize the word "angels" in accordance with its Greek application in the epistle. From Bradley Mellon, Ph.D. Hebrew scholar and friend, personal communication.

2 Francis Schaeffer, personal communication, 1977.

3 Hominids or Hominidae are allegedly members of a zoological family containing bipedal hominoids. Hominidea is a zoological superfamily supposedly containing gibbons, orangutans, chimpanzees, bonobos, gorillas, humans and many extinct species.

4 Elvio Angeloni, editor, *Physical Anthropology Annual Editions 93/94*, "Machiavellian Monkeys," by James Shreeve (Guilford, CN: The Dushkin Pub. Group, Inc., 1993), p. 44–47.

5 Douglas Futuyma, *Evolutionary Biology* (Sunderland, MA: Sinauer Assoc. Inc., 1986), p. 6.

6 Ibid., p. 2.

7 Phillip E. Johnson, *Darwin on Trial* (Washington, DC: Regnery, Gateway, 1991), p. 28.

8 Tim Berra, *Evolution and the Myth of Creationism* (Stanford, CA: Stanford University Press, 1990), p. viii, Preface.

9 Joshua A. Cuozzo, "Creation on Campus, Back to Genesis," ICR *Acts and Facts*, no. 98, February 1997, p. a–c.

10 Francis Darwin, *The Autobiography of Charles Darwin and Selected Letters* (New York, NY: Dover Pub. Inc., 1958), p. 244.

11 Jane R. Eisner, "Teens in Crisis," *The Philadelphia Inquirer*, June 6, 1999, editorial page, p. E6.

12 Will Durant, *The Story of Philosophy* (New York, NY: Simon and Schuster, 1953), p. 48.

13 Ibid., p. 48.

14 Ibid., p. 74.

15 Jack Cuozzo, *Buried Alive* (Green Forest, AR: Master Books, 1998), p. 132.

16 Angeloni, *Physical Anthropology Anual Editions 93/94*, "Dim Forest, Bright Chimps," by Christophe Boesch and Hedwig Boesch-Acherman, p.110–113.

17 E. Trinkaus and P. Shipman, *The Neandertals* (New York, NY: Alfred A. Knopf, Inc., 1992), p. 14.

18 Lord Rosebery, *Napoleon, The Last Phase* (New York, NY: Jonathan Cape and Harrison Smith, 1900), p. 191.

19 Donald Johanson and Blake Edgar, *From Lucy to Language* (New York, NY: Simon and Schuster, Editions, 1996), p. 18.

20 *Encyclopedia Britannica Book of the Year, 1979*, "Engineering Projects," Moffat (Chicago, IL: 1979), p. 354.
     Encyclopedia Britannica Book of the Year, 1979, "Environment," C.L. Boyle (Chicago, IL: 1979), p. 364.

21 Francis Schaeffer and C. Everett Koop *Whatever Happened to the Human Race?* (Old Tappan, NJ: F.H. Revell Co., 1979), p. 210.

22 Ibid., p. 210.
23 Meredith Wadman, "U.S. Senate Gets Tough on Animal Activists," *Nature*, vol. 399, no. 6735 (June 3, 1999): p. 397.
24 Robert Koenig, "European Researchers Grapple With Animal Rights," *Science*, vol. 284, no. 5420 (June 4, 1999): p. 1604–1606.
25 Ibid.
26 Angeloni, *Physical Anthropology Annual Editions 93/94,* "Jane Goodall and Flo," by Sy Montgomery, p. 75–81.
27 Cuozzo, *Buried Alive*, p. 106.
28 Angeloni, *Physical Anthropology Annual Editions 93/94,* "Interview Biruté Galdikas," by Don Lassem, p. 67–74.
29 A. Whiten, J. Goodall, W.C. McGrew, T. Nishida, V. Reynolds, Y. Sugiyama, C.E.G. Tutin, R.W. Wrangham, and C. Boesch, "Cultures in Chimpanzees," Letters to Nature, *Nature*, vol. 399, no. 6737 (June 17, 1999): p. 682–685.
30 Frans de Waal, "Cultural Primatology Comes of Age," *Nature*, vol. 399, no. 6737 (June 17, 1999): p. 635–636.
31 Richard Leakey and Roger Lewin, *Origins* (New York, NY: E.P. Dutton, Sequoia-Elsevier Pub Co., 1977), p. 8.
32 Modern German form is "tal"; the "h" has been dropped. However, I follow the older usage of Wilton M. Krogman, Chris Stringer, and Ian Tattersall.
33 Trinkaus and Shipman, *The Neandertals*, p. 6.
34 Cuozzo, *Buried Alive.*
35 Leonard Hayflick, *How and Why We Age* (New York, NY: Random House, 1994), p. 15.
    S. Olshansky, B. Carnes, and C. Cassel, "In Search of Methuselah: Estimating the Upper Limits to Human Longevity," *Science,* 250 (November 2, 1990): p. 634–640.
36 Today the section of anthropology concerned with human evolutionary studies is called paleoanthropology with the main emphasis on human paleontology (human ancestor remains). It includes the study of Paleolithic archeology, sometimes cultural anthropology, geological studies of sites, sometimes primate evolution.
37 Trinkaus and Shipman, *The Neandertals*, p. 103.

Chapter 4

THE DENIAL OF THE OBVIOUS

John D. Morris

We seem at last to have a unified theory — although a complex one inevitably, as evolution itself is a complex interaction of different processes — which is capable of facing all the classic problems of the history of life and of providing a causalistic solution of each.

This is not to say that the whole mystery [i.e., of evolution, ed.] has been plumbed to its core or even that it ever will be. The ultimate mystery is beyond the reach of scientific investigation, and probably of the human mind. There is neither need nor excuse for postulation of nonmaterial intervention in the origin of life, the rise of man, or any other part of the long history of the material cosmos. Yet the origin of that cosmos and the causal principles of its history remain unexplained and inaccessible to science. Here is hidden the First Cause sought by theology and philosophy. The First Cause is not known and I suspect that it never will be known to living man. We may, if we are so inclined, worship it in our own ways, but we certainly do not comprehend it.[1]

Although each has many variations, there are only

two basic world views which vie today for men's minds and hearts. Each purports to answer the big questions: Who am I? Where did I come from? What is the meaning to life? Where am I going? As mutually exclusive views of everything, only one of them can be right.

The traditional view is the biblical view, which holds that all things were created by an all-powerful and all-knowing Creator God transcendent to the universe. The Creator designed and made all things and now wisely governs His masterpiece. He created man "in His own image" with great worth and purpose and made communication and fellowship between God and man possible. Mankind's goal would be to live in harmony with his Creator, to bring Him glory and to enjoy Him forever.

The other world view holds that the universe is self-created, that natural processes, unthinking and impersonal, were the agents behind it all. No supernatural processes, (i.e., creation) were involved. Mankind, the highest evolved natural product can find worth only as conferred by himself and others. All deeds and goals can only be measured as to how they relate to this present natural world, to ourselves and to our posterity or, to put it more bluntly, survival and reproduction.

These two ways of thinking could hardly be more different. Tragically, the biblical creationist monotheistic view, once considered intuitively obvious, has largely been abandoned by the Western world, and adopted in its place has been the naturalistic pantheistic, evolutionary view. Before we chronicle the denial of what once was obvious, and the acceptance of what seems to us bizarre and degrading, let us fully examine the biblical view.

Creation, in the Beginning

The Bible tells us, "In the beginning, God created the heaven and the earth" (Gen. 1:1; KJV).

It goes on to explain, "In six days the LORD made

heaven and earth, the sea, and all that in them is, and rested the seventh day:" (Exod. 20:11).

What was God's evaluation of His creative handiwork? "And God saw every thing that He had made, and, behold, it was very good" (Gen. 1:31). God, the Master Designer, fashioned His created universe with intricate and beautiful design. This "very good" creation was mature and functioning from the start, with all of its systems in balance and accomplishing their purposes.

On day 1 of creation week, He began time and created space and matter. Then He brought forth light and separated the light from the darkness, providing a day/night cycle on planet Earth.

On day 2 He separated the waters which were above the atmosphere, from the waters which were below the atmosphere, preparing planet Earth to be self-sustaining and able to support life.

On day 3 He called the continents up from the ocean, blanketed them with topsoil and caused plants of all kinds to grow. These plants, lacking both blood and the breath of life, were created as food for living animals which were to be created later.

On day 4 He placed the sun in the sky as a permanent light source, bathing the earth in energy. He put the moon in the sky to give light at night and continually freshen the oceans by tidal action. He put the stars in the heavens to be used for timekeeping and direction, and placed light from these stars on the way to earth, so that once he was created on day 6, man would be able to utilize them.

On day 5 God continued to prepare the earth for habitation by man by filling the ocean with living creatures of all kinds. He also created the flying creatures, many with incredible beauty to adorn the newly formed continents.

On day 6 He created the land animals with great variety to live in every possible ecological niche with great variety in size and habit. Possessing breath, blood, and consciousness, these were truly "living creatures."

The crowning achievement of creation week was the creation of man in God's own image. Quantitatively superior to and qualitatively distinct from the animals, mankind, male and female, adequately represented God's image. This "image" consists primarily of aspects of the spiritual, emotional, volitional, and mental character of man. With the creation of mankind the creation was truly "finished," and God rested on the seventh day.

The animals, the plants, and mankind were all created "after their kind" as noted no less than ten times in Genesis chapter 1. God knew what each kind was to be like and He created them "after that kind" and did not fashion them by modifying previously existing kinds. He created each kind with the reproductive ability to procreate that kind, although with genetic ability to vary widely within the kind. For instance, we see a wide variety of "dogs," including wolves, coyotes, and domestic breeds, all stemming from the original dog "kind," but not from some other "kind."

Mankind was placed in charge of the creation and given the mandate to observe it, understand it, and utilize it for man's good and God's glory. They were placed in the Garden of Eden with every need supplied, including their needs for meaningful employment and fellowship with God. They were told to be fruitful, multiply, and fill the earth, ruling over it as God's stewards. Adam and Eve were in perfect harmony with one another, with creation, and with their Creator. In that "very good" world, there was no sickness or death and, most of all, no sin. Furthermore, they were endowed with the ability to reproduce God's image, and to fill the earth with their offspring.

As Creator, God had the authority to set the rules for their life and lifestyle. They were told that violating His one restriction would result in the death penalty. Tragically, before they even had time to obediently conceive and bear children they rejected God's authority and chose His punishment. Even more tragically, that sinful nature, that compulsion to rebel and make wrong choices, has passed to every one of Adam's descendants.

The next few chapters of Genesis explain how they were driven from the Garden to live in a world now full of sin and death. Soon their myriad descendants were so rebellious against God's authority that He chose to wash the creation clean with a great Flood in the days of Noah and start again with Noah and his descendants.

This year-long, mountain-covering, global Flood totally restructured the surface of the planet — eroding the continents here, re-depositing sediments there, raising mountains, and down-warping valleys. That year-long cataclysmic judgment completely re-worked the beautiful pre-Flood world, replacing it with a destroyed remnant. All land animals and all men not on board the ark of Noah perished in that Flood, as did untold billions of sea creatures and plants.

The restructuring of planet Earth left its effects, and the world following the Flood was quite different, with harsh climates and devastating geologic and meteorologic processes. Gradually, however, that world was refilled with plants and animals, each adapting to new niches and environments. Today we see a world maintaining a fragile balance, although with many residual catastrophes.

As they left the ark, Noah and his family were told to migrate and fill the earth with their descendants, but they chose instead to rebel and stay together. God, however, would not allow His plan to be abandoned, and confounded their languages, forcing them to migrate to all corners of the globe. As the various language groups migrated away from Babel, they adapted to local environmental conditions, acquiring characteristics suited to that area. We now recognize these language groups as nations, tribes, and ethnic peoples, each with certain abilities and technologies, but each equally dominated by the tendency to choose sin and the refusal to submit to the Creator's authority.

The Promise

Thankfully, the loss of the Edenic paradise is not the last chapter of the story, for as Adam and Eve were driven from the Garden of Eden, the Creator promised that His purposes in creation would not be ultimately thwarted. He prophesied that of their descendants would come one who would forever vanquish the enemy of God and His creation. This chosen "seed of the woman" (Gen. 3:15) would pay sin's penalty for those who had rejected God, and ultimately restore fellowship between the Creator and His fallen creation. This work of redemption and restoration was fully accomplished by the Lord Jesus Christ through His substitutionary death on the cross and resurrection from the dead. This restoration has not, however, been fully realized and today we see the creation groaning for the ultimate restitution of paradise on earth (Rom. 8:20–22).

The sweet fellowship intended between man and God has been broken, but God has not left us without a witness. He created in each one of us a conscience, the innate intuitive knowledge of right and wrong, a moral compass to assist us in choosing what would please Him. He gave us an amazing revelation in nature such that all we see around us, properly understood, points to an omniscient Designer/Creator behind it all. Furthermore, since all that we see now is not "very good," no longer in perfect balance and harmony, but only a judged and flooded remnant of the original creation, it bears eloquent testimony to the wages of sin. If the blinders have been removed from our eyes we see that nature demands a supernatural Creator. We observe a continual downward spiral of nature to a lesser and lesser degree of complexity, giving us clear testimony to a cursed creation, and testifying that today's natural processes could never have been the innovative and integrative processes which formed the "very good" creation in the beginning. We see plant and animal types still totally distinct from all other plant and animal types, bearing strong testimony to their separate origins. We see extensive rock units, the results of continent-wide catastrophic processes in the past, full of the fossils of plants and animals, creatures which died in a massive watery cataclysm, much greater than any mass killings occurring today. The evidence that the Creator has left for us is so "clearly seen" that if we do not see it we are "without excuse" (Rom. 1:20) and "willingly ignorant" (2 Pet. 3:6) of the facts.

But most of all, the Creator has communicated with His creation through His written Word and we can have full confidence in its reliability. In it are contained hundreds of prophecies, many of which have been already precisely fulfilled. There are many internal claims in this Book affirming that the human authors who penned it were divinely inspired, and even though hundreds of years separated the individual writers, the Book exhibits perfect internal consistency without contradiction. The Book contains many amazing scientific insights fully verified by modern observation. Truly our Bible is God's Word to His creation, containing all we need to know to understand Him and His creation, to build a fruitful life, and to live reunited with Him for eternity.

In order to answer the big questions of life: Who am I? Where did I come from? Where am I going? etc., we need to develop a fully biblical world view. The foundation for this world view is found in these four great worldwide events: the recent creation of all things in six days, the curse on all of creation due to man's rebellion, the global watery catastrophe in Noah's day, and the confusion of tongues at the Tower of Babel. On this foundation must be built an understanding of Christ's work on the cross, the role of the Church, and His consummation of all things in eternity. A proper understanding of these four great world-changing events of the long-ago past is essential if we are to properly understand the world around us today and in the future.

Where could one look in the universe and see something whose ultimate origin was not creation? What observation could one make of a process or an entity, which is not suffering under the penalty of Adam's sin and the curse on all of his domain? What rock unit or mountain chain on planet Earth was not affected by the global flood of Noah's day? What nation or ethnic group did not descend from those dispersed from the Tower of Babel? Even though they are absolutely foundational, it is these four great events, which are most neglected in Christian circles and denied in naturalistic circles today, leading not only to error but great folly.

A denial of supernatural creation will lead one to assume that natural processes are behind it all. A denial of the Curse might then lead one to think that the ubiquitous disintegration that we see could somehow be innovative. A denial of the catastrophic Flood would then lead him to think that long ages of slow and gradual processes could somehow add up to all the changes necessary to form the present structure of the earth. Finally, a denial of the separation of language groups at the Tower of Babel might lead people to think that some ethnic groups are more highly evolved than others.

Needless to say, our society is dominated by thinking like this. The steps which have been taken to bring about such a state bear our close examination.

The Rejection of the Creation of All Things

Consider the following oft-repeated quote from Sir Julian Huxley, who, until his death in 1975, was perhaps the world's leading spokesman for evolution and who, from his position as head of UNESCO at the United Nations, did much to unite the world under an evolutionary, humanistic banner.

> Darwin pointed out that no supernatural designer was needed; since natural selection could account for any known form of life, there was no room for a supernatural agency in its evolution . . . we can dismiss entirely all ideas of a supernatural overriding mind being responsible for the evolutionary process.[2]

The recent edition of the authoritative Encyclopedia Britannica informs us that:

> Darwin did two things: He showed that evolution was a fact contradicting literal interpretations of scriptural legends of creation and that its cause, natural selection, was automatic with no room for divine guidance or design.[3]

The design and complexity of living things is the most obvious evidence for creation, presenting an immense problem for evolution by natural processes. It has been noted that even the smallest single-celled organism is more engineered, more complex than a super computer. It takes an unusual abandonment of logic to conclude that intricately and efficiently designed systems can arise by unthinking random processes. Yet evolutionists for many years have made themselves believe that natural selection can somehow do this!

In Darwin's day it was thought that a living cell was a simple sac filled with fluid. Microscopes were insufficient to discern that the cell is intricately complex with a wide variety of organelles carrying out an amazing variety of functions. Each one of these subunits is itself composed of subunits which are themselves highly organized. Each subpart has a purpose, crucial to the functioning of the whole. Take away one part or incapacitate one function and the entire cell ceases to function. Some parts provide energy, some assimilate food, some excrete waste, some assist in the reproductive process — none is either simple or dispensable. Each is beyond the ability of modern science to duplicate or even fully understand.

The cell wall is itself incredibly well engineered, a selective barrier protecting the cell from outside invaders and yet allowing nutrients to cross. Furthermore, scientists continue to discover new complexities and new functions of the cell all the time. When will their insistence that it is all due to random processes be abandoned? It would be more scientific to claim that super-computers arose spontaneously from an explosion at an electronic parts store than to say the smallest single-celled organism could arise from non-living chemicals, just by chance random processes.

Of course, not even a computer with all of its hardware intact could function without software. In just the same manner, the cell has software directing its hardware to accomplish useful tasks. The late naturalist Carl Sagan, who fully believed that life arose from non-life strictly by natural processes once admitted:

> The information content of a simple cell has been established as around 10^{12} bits, comparable to about a hundred million pages of the Encyclopedia Britannica.[4]

And yet he was certain that this software package wrote itself!

The most articulate defender of such alleged naturalistic processes today is Oxford's Richard Dawkins. All the while insisting that life has no designer behind it, he still admits:

> There is enough information capacity in a single human cell to store the Encyclopedia Britannica, all 30 volumes of it, three or four

times over. I don't know the comparable figure for a willow seed or an ant, but it will be of the same order of staggeringness. There is enough storage capacity in the DNA of a single lily seed or a single salamander sperm to store the Encyclopedia Britannica 60 times over. Some species of the unjustly called "primitive" amoebas have as much information in their DNA as 1,000 Encyclopedia Britannicas.[5]

The fact that such illogic is accepted and even championed in evolutionary circles underscores our contention that this naturalistic view is held for world view reasons, not for scientific reasons.

Sir Fred Hoyle, one of the greatest scientists of the 20th century, investigated the possibility of life arising naturalistically from non-life. He started his investigation as a complete naturalist, but at the end he said:

> The chance that higher life forms might have arisen in this fashion is equivalent to the chance that a tornado sweeping through a junkyard might assemble a Boeing 747 from the materials therein.[6]

Containing more information than a CD-ROM, the DNA code is written in a language which modern scientists, with all of their attempts, have not been able to decipher. To an increasing degree, we can determine which sections of the DNA code address certain problems, but we don't really understand what they are saying. For instance, we know which suite of genes code for human insulin but why this particular suite of base pairs codes for insulin we do not know. We do know that, when that suite is inserted into a bacterium, it continues to produce human insulin which can be harvested and has been of life-saving value to countless diabetics. But knowing which page of the encyclopedia discusses insulin and being able to write it in the first place are two different things. We certainly could not have written these instructions from scratch. How dare arrogant scientists say it can happen by chance without a supernatural author?

The Bible tells us that God declared His completed creation "finished," and rested from His creative work, so that the process of creation is no longer taking place. The Creator is now "upholding all things by the word of His power" (Heb. 1:3). Nothing is now being either created or destroyed.

Science has discovered this truth and recognized its importance by imparting to it the status of law. The first law of thermodynamics, the basic, best-proven law of science, states that nothing is now being either created or destroyed. Things can change form, but the sum total of what exists remains the same. And yet, the universe and its tremendous quantities of matter and energy are all here. Therefore, they must have been created by processes and laws not now in operation. If anything should be obvious to scientists as exemplified in this most basic law of science, this is it. Why then do so many ignore this basic truth?

Several decades before Darwin, the Reverend William Paley argued conclusively for the necessity of a supernatural designer in his classic work *Natural Theology*. The clamor for a naturalistic origin of mankind and a denial of the Creator's authority had been in vogue long before Darwin, and Paley did his best to remind his colleagues of the obvious truth that design demands a designer.

His most famous analogy was that of the watch and the watchmaker. Suppose, he asked, one finds a watch out in a field far from any evidence of human presence? In a carefully worded, logical argument he showed that in spite of the fact that the watch was made up of smaller, less complex components, and even if it might be broken and no longer functioning, it still bore the unmistakable sign of a watchmaker. It could not have happened strictly by natural processes. We chuckle at the obvious nature of this conclusion, but then why don't we chuckle when England's eminent spokesman for evolution, Sir Richard Dawkins, publishes his book *The Blind Watchmaker* to insist that things much more complex than a watch can come about by natural processes?

> Paley's argument is made with passionate sincerity and is informed by the best biological scholarship of his day, but it is wrong, gloriously and utterly wrong. The analogy between telescope and eye, between watch and living organism, is false. All appearances to the contrary, the only watchmaker in nature is the blind forces of physics, albeit deployed in a very special way. A true watchmaker has foresight: he designs his cogs and springs, and plans their interconnections, with a future purpose in his mind's eye. Natural selection, the blind, unconscious, automatic process which Darwin discovered, and which we now know is the explanation for the existence and apparently purposeful form of all life, has no purpose in mind. It has no mind and no mind's eye. It does not plan for the future. It has no vision, no foresight, no sight at all. If it can be said to play the role of watchmaker in nature, it is the *blind* watchmaker. [7]

Charles Darwin was educated in a climate where Paley's arguments were recognized as intuitively true. But, as noted in another chapter, there was a strong undercurrent of scientific animosity toward God, which strove to reject the obvious truth of creation and the attendant submission to a creator's authority, in favor of some other more naturalistic mechanism. Many had even toyed with the idea of natural selection being responsible, but it was not until Charles Darwin published his book *Origin of Species* in 1859 that an appealing case for it was made.

Darwin admitted the weaknesses of natural selection, especially in accounting for the precisely designed organs in the human body, such as the human eye. In his book *Origin of Species*, he exclaimed:

> To suppose the eye with all of its inimitable contrivances for adjusting the focus to different distances, for admitting different amounts of light, and for the correction of spherical and chromatic aberration, could have been formed by natural selection, seems, I freely confess, *absurd* in the highest degree[8] (emphasis added).

But then he went on to explain how he thought it might have happened by imperceptibly small, naturally occurring steps.

But Darwin's insistence on strict naturalism (read anti-supernaturalism) was not well received by many of his scientific colleagues. As admitted in his memoirs and correspondence, it was for personal reasons that he had rejected the idea of a personal God and was thus forced into his naturalistic stance, often disregarding the obvious message of the scientific evidence. Not all scientists were the doctrinaire naturalist that he was. Consider the following quote from Darwin to an American evolutionist at Harvard by the name of Asa Gray. Gray was a theistic evolutionist, not a strictly naturalistic evolutionist like Darwin. In fact, he challenged Darwin's atheism, to which Darwin replied in a letter on May 22, 1860:

> I had no intention to write atheistically. But I own that I cannot see as plainly as others do, and as I should wish to do, evidence of design and beneficence on all sides of us. There seems to me too much misery in the world. I cannot

persuade myself that a beneficent and omnipotent God would have designedly created the ichneumonidae (i.e., parasite) with the express intention of their feeding within the living bodies of caterpillars, or that a cat should play with mice. Not believing this, I see no necessity in the belief that the eye was expressly designed.[9]

Thus, we see that Darwin's acceptance of evolution was not because of scientific reasons but for theological reasons. He plainly saw the prominence of death, pain, and suffering engulfing the living world. He saw extinction and mutation and cancer and parasites and rightly reasoned that the God of the Bible would not have created things in this fashion. But, as we have seen, the world that Darwin observed, and that we observe, is not the world as God created it. Refusing to acknowledge the effects of the Curse, and how Adam's rebellion ruined God's "very good" creation, he wrongly chose to deny God as Creator. His logic from that point on is sound. If there is no supernatural creator then natural processes are all that could have acted. Even though the resultant conclusions were, at times, admittedly "absurd," natural selection was his best guess.

His writings, based as they were on an illogical major premise, nevertheless provided the foes of supernaturalism a pseudo-scientific basis for their beliefs. This flawed thinking has continued to dominate science and education, the media, and public policy ever since.

The Rejection of the Curse on All of Creation

The Bible says that "the whole creation groaneth and travaileth in pain together until now" under the "bondage of corruption," of sin and its penalty, death (Rom. 8:22, 21). The physical and most obvious effect of Adam's rebellion was that the "very good" creation was made no longer very good. What had been sinless and disease-free, with every need amply provided, was no longer so.

In Genesis 3:14–19 God explained to Adam the penalty for what he had done and how it would cause all of the creation, which had been put under his stewardship, to come under Divine penalty. Adam was told that from that time on, the animals were cursed — the serpent more than the rest of the animals. Plants were cursed with thorns and thistles. Difficulty in surviving would be increased. Bearing children would no longer be a pleasurable experience, and marriage relationships were strained. Just as "the wages of sin is death" in Romans 6:23, so it was in Genesis. They had been told that they should not eat of the tree of the knowledge of good and evil, "For in the day that thou eatest thereof, thou shalt surely die" (literally, dying thou shalt die) (Gen. 2:17). After Adam rebelled, God promised that he would return unto the ground; "for dust thou art, and unto dust thou shalt return" (Gen. 3:19). Now everything dies — animals die, people die, inanimate objects deteriorate. Indeed, "the whole creation" is ruined by Adam's rebellion.

Furthermore, the Curse and its effects are not limited just to the earth, for the moon's orbit is decaying, the sun is burning out, the stars explode — such obvious reminders of the penalty for sin are all around us and inescapable. But remember that God did not curse the creation in a fit of vindictiveness, He did so to draw us back to His gracious provision for sin, the substitutionary death of His Son, Jesus Christ, on our behalf.

The Curse finds its way into biological systems, of course. Changes in the DNA — called mutations or birth defects — have all been harmful, or at best neutral. God's systems were highly designed and even after thousands of years of mutations, the design is still obvious, but the genetic load of mutations that animals and plants are carrying is large and growing. Many think this is the cause of the rapid increase in degenerative diseases being visited upon humankind. Things obviously cannot go on forever continuing to deteriorate like they are. The fact that they still function is evidence that they are not excessively old, for then they would have ceased to function. The fact that no genetic mutations (whether spontaneous or artificially induced) have ever been seen to produce lasting improvements is proof that modern processes could not have been involved in the origin of living things.

Mutations are still touted by evolutionists as the source of new species and innovative basic body plans, but not one new independent species, no longer interfertile with its supposed parent species, has ever been documented as resulting from either natural or artificial processes. What does result is extinction, with estimates of many species going extinct each year. Every observation we make is in the exact opposite direction from that which evolution by natural processes would predict. How can its advocates continue in good conscience to insist it be taught as fact?

This decay principle has been likewise recognized by science. It is called the second law of thermodynamics or, in some spheres, the second law of science. The second law applies to every system, isolated, closed, or open, and insists that the quality of order, information, or energy in that system will spontaneously decrease without a specific and directed method of harnessing incoming energy and applying it to useful ends. Photosynthesis and the DNA do this in plants, and thus plants can survive for a while, but incoming energy will not produce a more ordered DNA code nor could it have devised the intricate photosynthesis process in the first place. Thus, we can see that evolution by the processes which operate today is impossible. Evolution is against the law — scientific law, that is.

As we have seen, Darwin rejected the traditional Christian view that disease and suffering were due to the Curse, as have philosophers and naturalists before and since.

> You simply can't any longer say as tradi-
> tional Christians that death was God's punish-
> ment for sin. Death was around long before hu-
> man beings. Death is a necessary aspect of an
> evolutionary world.[10]

This might be excusable for one who is philosophi-
cally committed to naturalism, but what can we make of
professing Christians such as Barbour who aggressively
opt for the naturalistic view, who recognize that old-earth
thinking necessitates millions of years of death and suffering before man, and that Adam's world, which God
called "very good," was filled with disease and suffering
and death.

Death is not good! It was not part of the "very good"
creation at the beginning, nor will it be in the new heavens
and new earth where "God shall wipe away all tears from
their eyes; and there shall be no more death, neither sorrow, nor crying, neither shall there be any more pain: for
the former things are passed away" (Rev. 21:4). Surely the
biblical warning promising "woe to them who call good
evil and evil good" (Isa. 5:20) applies to Christians as well
as non-Christians.

Many have tried to dismiss the implications of the
second law, but as the authors of a classic textbook on
thermodynamics have stated, "We see the second law of
thermodynamics as a description of the prior and continuing work of a Creator, who also holds the answer to
our future destiny and that of the universe."

> Does the second law of thermodynamics
> apply to the universe as a whole? Are there pro-
> cesses unknown to us that occur somewhere in
> the universe, such as "continual creation," that
> have a decrease in entropy associated with them,
> and thus offset the continual increase in entropy
> that is associated with the natural processes that

are known to us? If the second law is valid for the universe (we of course do not know if the universe can be considered as an isolated system), how did it get in the state of low entropy? On the other end of the scale, if all processes known to us have an increase in entropy associated with them, what is the future of the natural world as we know it? Quite obviously, it is impossible to give conclusive answers to these questions on the basis of the second law of thermodynamics alone. However, we see the second law of thermodynamics as a description of the prior and continuing work of a Creator, who also holds the answer to our future destiny and that of the universe.[11]

In spite of the obvious anti-evolutionary implications of the second law, many evolutionists have brashly claimed that the second law does not apply to living systems which are open to outside energy. In public they have refused to acknowledge the additional requirements for spontaneous increase in order, but privately were concerned by this situation. This became obvious when scientist Ilya Prigogine was awarded a Nobel Prize for "solving" the problem.

What I see Prigogine doing is giving legitimization to the process of evolution — self organization under conditions of change.[12]

Prigogine showed that in certain very low temperature processes there can be local and temporary "structures" produced spontaneously, but these were hardly more ordered than a swirl in a hot cup of coffee. Nevertheless, evolutionists responded gleefully, celebrating that the problem had been solved. Order can arise spontaneously in disordered systems, therefore evolution is proven, they seem to be saying.

> In classical thermodynamics, the dissipation of energy in heat transfer, friction, and the like was always associated with waste. Prigogine's concept of a dissipative structure introduced a radical change in this view by showing that in open systems dissipation becomes a source of order.[13]

But despite such enthusiastic claims by evolutionists, such minimally "ordered" systems, which form in accordance with the laws of physics, have nothing to do with the origin of highly complex systems like living cells or intelligent information codes like the DNA, in violation of known laws. Despite their protests, the problem has not been solved and thermodynamics still provides an insurmountable barrier to real evolution.

But this hasn't stopped the religious, naturalistic evolutionist from over-extending the meager evidence and proposing what has come to be known as chaos theory. This concept, highly mathematical and rather otherworldly, supposes that the few very small and temporary increases in order from "chaos" that we do see can be magnified into major increases in order. A common cliché is that a butterfly flapping its wings in Beijing, China, could generate a hurricane in New York City. Must this type of perversion of thinking continue to be passed off as science? Surely both science and logic faired better when Christians roamed the earth.

The Rejection of the Cataclysmic Flood of Noah's Day

The Bible describes the flood of Noah's day as worldwide in scope and catastrophic in effect. No place on planet Earth could have escaped its impact. While we can't go back in time to see what the Flood accomplished, we can list what we would expect to find in the geologic record if the Flood occurred as described in the Bible, and then check that list against the geologic record to see if it matches.

Based on the biblical description of the Flood, we would expect to discover that cataclysmic processes operated on a very large scale with energy levels and rates far exceeding anything that has operated since that time. And that is exactly what we do find. We see a record of erosion, re-deposition of sediments, volcanism, mountain uplift, and fossilization operating in the past on scales which far eclipse those operating today.

Science in Europe began to flower following the Reformation, and those interested in geology recognized the flood of Noah's day as the causative agent in depositing strata and fossilizing plants and animals. Many things were poorly understood, but in general the past event of the Flood was the key to understanding what they could see in the present. This included coal beds in England, fossils of sea creatures in elevated regions, and the rugged Alps.

But the forces of naturalism were active in the geological sciences. In the late 1700s James Hutton advocated that the world was extremely old, not just the few thousand years indicated in Scripture. Sir Charles Lyell amplified Hutton's views in the 1820s and 1830s. His slogan, "The present is the key to the past," mirrored his contention that only those processes which operate today, operating at rates similar to today, have acted throughout the past and are responsible for all that we see. His was a specific denial of the clear biblical teaching of recent creation and global Flood. Lyell marshaled many seemingly convincing arguments for long ages to account for the chalk cliffs of Dover, the gorge of the Niagara River, etc. His concept of "uniformity" was not well received by the scientists of the day who recognized that the geologic record spoke eloquently of catastrophic processes.

He was, however, well received by the theologians of the day, particularly in the Church of England. With little dissent, they renounced the biblical doctrines of creation, young earth, and global Flood, and even adopted varying

views of evolution, thus paving the way for Darwin to follow in 1859. While the scientists argued that a monstrous
Flood could accomplish a great deal of geologic work in
a short period of time, theologians wondered where such
a volume of water would come from and how Noah could
have gotten all the animals on board the ark. Without
answers to these questions, easily answerable today, they
were willing to give up even the doctrine of the inerrancy
of Scripture, thus leading the Church into great darkness.

Actually, the Bible predicts that this error would
dominate the last days in which the creed of "scoffers"
would be, "Where is the promise of His coming? For since
the fathers fell asleep all things continue as they were from
the beginning of creation" (2 Pet. 3:3–4). Thus, present
processes operating as they are now have always operated
from the beginning and are responsible for all that we see.
Such a beautiful prediction and description of the mod-
ern-day concept of uniformitarianism could only come
from the author of Scripture, and therefore the identifica-
tion of its advocates as "scoffers" is appropriate.

The passage goes on to say "For this they willingly
are ignorant of, that by the word of God the heavens were
of old, and the earth standing out of the water and in the
water, by which the world that then was, being overflowed
with water, perished" (2 Pet. 3:5–6).

Thus, we see that these latter day scoffers are willingly ignorant of creation and the Flood. They see the
evidence for design, they see the evidence for catastrophic
flooding, and they choose not to acknowledge it. They
are willingly ignorant of the evidence.

Lyell even resorted to deception to prove his point.
At Niagara Falls, he was told by local landowners that the
falls were eroding upriver at a rate of about five feet per
year. Thus, the seven-mile long (35,000 feet) river gorge
could have been eroded in just a few thousand years. But
Lyell reported the erosion rate at one foot per year; thus

the gorge required about 35,000 years to erode, more time than the biblical chronologies allow. But what of the Flood, and even greater erosion rates? Denying the truth of this historical event led him and many who followed to conclude wrongly that modern processes over long ages were responsible.

Interestingly enough, catastrophism is making a comeback in the modern geologic world. As is now widely admitted, the concept of uniformity is impotent, totally incapable of producing the geologic record of the past as we see it today. Now geologists are quite willing to talk about continents moving around or meteorite bombardment killing all the dinosaurs or massive volcanic episodes. These "neo-catastrophists" do not acknowledge these catastrophes as comprising the flood of Noah's day, but as separate catastrophes separated by millions of years. These trends are encouraging, but there is still need for a recognition that all these separate catastrophes were actually components of the global cataclysm of the flood in Noah's day.

The Rejection of the Confusion of Languages at Babel

The apostle Paul reminded the intellectuals of his day assembled on Mars Hill that God had "made of one blood all nations of men to dwell on all the face of the earth, and hath determined the times before appointed, and the bounds of their habitation" (Acts 17:26). All men trace their lineage back to Adam and Eve and more recently to Noah and his family, separated into language groups at the Tower of Babel. Today we see myriads of nations and tongues and tribes, all merely varieties of the original family.

Interestingly enough, 70 language groups/nations are mentioned as having migrated from the Tower of Babel once the languages were confounded. While there are many more languages than that in existence today, they group into language families numbering on this same order. Evidently, some basic languages have gone extinct and some amalgamated into other languages, but the present number of basic languages testifies to the truth of the Genesis account.

These separate languages may have caused nations to war throughout history, but the inescapable point is that we are all of one race, the human race.

Conversely, the concept of ethic racial groups is an evolutionary one. In fact, Darwin's book, *Origin of Species,* was subtitled *The Preservation of Favored Races in the Struggle for Life.* He considered the different ethnic groups to be subspecies with some more highly evolved than others. For example, he felt that the Turkish people, who at that time ruled much of the Middle East and Asia, were an inferior race and would be dispossessed by the Caucasian race. He considered the black African peoples to be the lowest (that is, least evolved) among human "races."

Darwin's main promoter on the European continent was Ernst Haeckel, author of the failed concept of embryonic recapitulation, to be discussed elsewhere in this book. Haeckel was a thorough-going racist and used evolution to justify his views. As a German, he was especially interested in promoting the Aryan race as a super race. This led directly to World War I and then to World War II as Hitler utilized these concepts. Hitler's well-known racial hatred of the people of Israel led to the unthinkable Holocaust, but he was only carrying out the dictates of "survival of the fittest" by weeding out those he felt were unfit.

Racism was not unique to Hitler's Germany, but had long infected America's shores. Even now, though slavery has been abolished for over a century, racism still dominates many minds. It must be replaced by biblical truth. We must return to the biblical view that all of mankind goes back to Noah and back to Adam. All men are sinners and in desperate need of a Savior. Jesus Christ has come to die to pay the penalty for the sin of individuals from every tongue and tribe and nation. There will come a time when the saved remnant out of every tongue and tribe and nation will gather around His throne to praise Him for all eternity. There is no room in Christian doctrine for racism. It is an evolutionary inference with serious and devastating consequences.

Another great movement alive today rejects God's plan for separate nations and separate languages. Western nations in particular are consumed with the idea of a one-world government, and even the reinstitution of a world language, in direct violation of the Creator's mandate for the world. This seems to be paving the way for the predicted despicable world ruler in the last days.

The Modern Creation Movement

The naturalistic view held sway in the Western world for several decades. During its tenure of monopoly, biology was dominated by evolution, geology by uniformitarianism, and the Church by compromise. In many ways this has begun to change. The more we learn of the amazing complexity of living things to even the smallest single-celled organism, the more it is recognized that natural processes could never produce what we see. The more we learn of the geologic evidence existing as it does on such a wide scale with a catastrophic signature, the more it is recognized that present processes were not the cause. As more powerful telescopes look to the heavens, stellar evolution concepts must rely on ever more fanciful ideas. In response, many evolutionists are becoming more willing to talk about intelligent design, and geologists about catastrophism. A number of important astronomers are desperately looking for some way to modify the big bang to make it workable. Far too many denominational leaders and seminary professors, however, remain mired in compromise with these worldly systems.

Into this fray has come the resurgence of biblical and

scientific creationism. Beginning with the publication of the classic work *The Genesis Flood* in 1961 by Henry Morris and John Whitcomb, a revival of interest in creation thinking has blossomed. Since that time, well over a hundred creationist organizations have been formed, and there are now well over a thousand fully credentialed creationist scientists recognizing the scientific superiority of creation, along with tens of millions of people identifying themselves as creationists.

It is possible once again to talk about the inerrancy of Scripture, now that creation, too, can be defended. Furthermore, it is possible to engage a skeptical scientific public with the truths of young-earth creation and global Flood. It is possible to successfully debate the issue on university campuses. It is legitimate to expose the religious underpinnings of the evolutionary, naturalistic world view and demand that this religion be removed from our school systems. Many scholars are abandoning naturalistic evolution in the face of this evidence. Unfortunately, as people leave evolution, many are going into the New Age movement.

In the midst of it all are creation advocates who act as standard bearers, calling the Church back to a belief in all of Scripture. It is often at a creation-science seminar that both Christians and non-Christians are reminded of the accuracy of God's Word and the authority of the Creator over their lives and lifestyle. Careful creationist presentation of the doctrine of salvation, showing how the "very good" creation was ruined by sin, but how the Creator himself has died to pay sin's penalty to restore fallen creation to fellowship with Him, has elicited true revival in many hearts and churches. The future may be uncertain, but one thing is sure, things will never go back to the way they were. Christians have begun to reclaim lost ground.

The New Heavens and New Earth

The revival of interest in biblical and scientific creationism comes not a moment too soon, for time grows short. "Scoffers" — uniformitarian biologists and geologists — still dominate the intellectual scene, and open rejection of biblical thinking is still rampant. But we know that these things will shortly come to an end. We are told that someday "the heavens being on fire shall be dissolved, and the elements shall melt with fervent heat. Nevertheless, we, according to His promise, look for new heavens and a new earth, wherein dwelleth righteousness" (2 Pet. 3:12–13). With creation restored, the Curse removed, and the Creator visibly reigning on His throne, truth will once again flourish. Until then, much remains to be done.

Endnotes

1 George Gaylord Simpson, *The Meaning of Evolution* (New Haven, CT: Yale University Press, 1967).

2 Sol Tax, editor, *Issues in Evolution* (Chicago, IL: University of Chicago Press, 1960).

3 *The New Encyclopedia Britannica,* "The Theory of Evolution," 1986, Vol. 18, p. 996.

4 *The New Encyclopedia Britannica,* "Life," 1986, Vol. 22, p. 987.

5 Richard Dawkins, *The Blind Watchmaker* (New York, NY: W.W. Norton, 1986), p. 115–116.

6 "Hoyle on Evolution," *Nature,* vol. 294 (November 12,1981): p. 105.

7 Dawkins, *The Blind Watchmaker.*

8 Charles Darwin, *The Origin of Species* (London: A.L. Burt, 1859), p. 168.

9 Charles Darwin in a letter to Asa Gray, May 22, 1860.

10 Ian Barbour, scientist, 1999 winner of the Templeton Prize for Progress in Religion.

11 Richard Sonntag and Gordon J. Van Wylen, *Fundamentals of Classical Thermodynamics* (New York, NY: Wiley. 1986), p. 1236–1237.

12 *Chemical and Engineering News,* "The Social Thermodynamics of Ilya Prigogine," by Wil Lepkowski (New York, NY: Bantam, 1979), p. 30.

13 Fritjof Capra, *The Web of Life* (New York, NY: Anchor Books, 1996), p. 89.

Chapter 5

CULTURE CHANGE:
THE CREATION BACKGROUND

Carl Wieland

Well, I think Christianity is not much good, anyway. I'm drawn to religions like Buddhism or Islam," said the young geology student. She had telephoned the Australian radio station on which I was speaking live on Bible/science issues. Lacking the equipment for talk-back, the station was taking calls off-air; hers had been put through to my colleague, Warwick.

"Tell me, Miss," said Warwick. "When you have children, say you could choose any country in the world to bring them up in, which would you choose?"

"Australia, of course," she replied.

Warwick shot back, "If it couldn't be Australia, what would be your next choice?"

"Umm . . . America, I guess . . . or maybe England."

"And if that isn't possible?"

"Well," she replied, hesitating, "probably Germany . . . or Switzerland."

This went on for a little while, and then my colleague

said, "Miss, do you realize that of all of the countries you listed, not one was Buddhist or Islamic?" I had to revert to the microphone at that point, but it wasn't hard to see where things were heading. In addition to the lack of Buddhist or Islamic countries in her list, I noted that it was composed of countries which, despite the blatant secularism of many of them today, all historically shared a strong Christian social foundation.

You might want to try that approach on others sometime. It's actually not a bad way to start talking about the things of God — most people are interested in a conversation which refers to their children, even if only hypothetically. Of course, our young lady's choices were neither unusual nor surprising. Not even the most vehement Christian-bashers would prefer to bring their children up in Iran, Burma, Saudi Arabia, or the like.

Hardly any would make a connection between their choice of countries and the Bible. I was discussing this with a young man who at first refused to accept that his "country list" had anything to do with Christian heritage. "In South America, Christianity conquered the local religions and reigned supreme, churches and crosses are everywhere," he said. "But I can't think of too many South American countries I would want my children brought up in, either."

I pointed out that the link was not about churchianity or public displays of "religion," but the real life-and-culture-transforming power of the Christ of the Bible. It was about a way of thinking which was based on the Bible, and which had changed the lives of millions, who had in turn affected others, so that even unbelievers were swept up in the positive benefits which flowed from it. It was easy to show how the countries he had chosen for his children's upbringing had, like those on our geology student's list, all been at some stage powerfully affected by the Reformation and its strong biblical emphasis, whereas this had bypassed the South American ones he had rejected.

The reasons for such "country" choices have, on the surface, nothing to do with Christianity. They involve such things as economic opportunity (associated with a high level of technology), reasonable expectations of justice in a society ruled by law, freedom of thought and expression, the relative absence of corruption, the dignity of the individual, human rights, and so on. So why are high scores in all these things so strongly clustered in countries touched by the Bible?

If those of us of Western European extraction are honest, our thinking on such matters is often associated with a degree of racism. We find it unremarkable that the societies which are the most "advanced" in their economies, their technology, or their degree of "civilized" behavior tend to be those which are the most like "us." This is why most westerners tend to see the correlation of such desirable cultural traits with the Bible as incidental. They think it is because Western Europe just happens to have had a strong Christian/Protestant heritage. A more likely cause for the dominance of cultures with a Western European heritage, they think, is that the same countries were also historically at the forefront of the development of science and technology, and it is these which are seen as the true liberators of mankind. And of course "our kind of people" would naturally be the first ones to discover science, wouldn't they?

The reality is, though, that matters of racial or genetic endowment have little to do with the distribution of "favored" countries and cultures. (Hardly surprising, since the real history of the world, given in the Bible, shows that we are all of "one blood" anyway. Which is consistent with the recent discovery of the astonishing genetic closeness of all so-called "races.")

It was, in fact, the Bible, rediscovered and unchained at the Reformation, and the Gospel preaching which flowed from its pages, which led naturally and consistently to all of the reasons (not just science and technology) for virtually everyone tending to rate cultures with such a heritage more highly than those without.

This is all-important to our theme, by the way. Most readers would share our concern about the downhill direction of our culture. Our title has, I imagine, an attraction not just because of its dinosaur imagery, but because we look back with fondness to the recent past in our Western nations, when indeed more Christians seemed to "roam the earth." Though things were far from perfect then, even most unbelievers see the recent changes in our Western culture as unfavorable. And everyone knows of the concomitant decline in Christian influence. It is the correlation between the two that is poorly understood, even by most Christians.

In the United States, where evangelical Christians make up a huge percentage of the voting population, most of them stand perplexed at their corporate powerlessness to influence popular culture as they once did. Hundreds of millions of dollars have been poured by them into organizations to fight the symptoms of this decline — soaring abortion, pornography, senseless lawlessness — to no avail.

Even a brief exploration of the links between secular culture and the Bible will help us to better understand the foundational causes of the decline.

Science and Technology

Though many secular academics have long ago made the connection, even most Christians are still unaware of the way in which it was the Bible, rediscovered and refocused upon at the time of the Reformation, which led directly to the subsequent explosion of science and technology in Western Europe. Western Europeans "stole a march" in these areas (and their associated economic benefits), not because of any innate superiority, but because their culture was blessed with a way of thinking about the world which happened to be right.

We look at the countries of Islam today, and often forget how advanced some of the great thinkers and scholars of the Arabic world were. Some of the finest mathematicians of antiquity were among their ranks, not to mention physicians. Yet modern science was not born there. The brilliance of the ancient Greeks needs no introduction — yet the way of thinking and investigating that we call science did not arise from their midst. Many ancient civilizations came close to making the leap; the Chinese made numerous discoveries and inventions long before the West. But the few intermittent signs of gestation of scientific thinking in such cultures led only to a series of stillbirths.

Modern scientific thinking is so ingrained in us that we find it hard to see how people could think otherwise. It seems obvious to us that there is an objective reality "out there," ripe for us to uncover ever more and deeper knowledge of the way it works. We take for granted the idea that the world functions according to regular, unchanging laws that we can rely on absolutely, and thus harness for our benefit.

But imagine someone brought up in a culture which believed that within every rock or tree there was an individual spirit. What motivation would they have for believing that there was an innate orderliness or predictability about the way in which rocks and trees behaved?

What if you had been brought up in a culture which believed, as so many did and some still do, that the universe was an illusion of the mind, or was itself one big thought? What sense is there in investigating something which may not even really, objectively exist? Why even think of looking for regular laws which govern the behavior of a universe which, being mind, could change its mind?

By contrast, the notion of a Creator God independent of His creation more readily leads to the idea of lawfulness; the maker of nature is presumably the ruler of nature.

Thus, creation-based cultures were always more likely to discover the creation's lawfulness. But all Creator concepts are not the same. The law-giving God of the Christian Bible stands unique in the extent of His lawfulness.

Jesus Christ, God the Son who made all things (Col. 1:16) is "the same yesterday, today and forever" (Heb. 13:8; NKJV), so His created laws can be expected to be likewise unchanging.

Had you been raised in ancient Greece, you would have been saturated with talk of "gods," but they could not be depended upon to ordain an unchanging lawfulness in the world. For one thing, they were not the ultimate reality, in the way the Creator God of the Bible is. They did not always exist, but had themselves evolved from some pre-existent reality, some primordial ooze. And even though they had some sway over the forces of nature, Zeus and the gang on Olympus were renowned for being capricious, even deceptive. So things fall down today — who is to say that tomorrow, the gods will not decree that they go upwards? Or fall at a different rate?

If you saw something in a rock that looked like a fish, since common sense says that fish don't live in rocks, it was probably the gods up to tricks. The medieval idea of fossils being manufactured by God or the devil to fool us or test our faith did not derive from the Bible, but was inherited from Greek thought. Incidentally, Nicolaus Steno, the founding father of modern geology and stratigraphy, avoided such ideas in his correct reasoning about the connection between fossils and the processes of sedimentation. Like the founders of virtually all scientific disciplines, he was a believer in literal Genesis creation and a world Flood. Such beliefs were not incidental to the rise of science, but a crucial part of it.

One of the fundamental principles upon which modern science is built is the general uniformity of natural law, also called the "non-capriciousness of nature," i.e., nature is not fickle or erratic. The whole of experimental science would be pointless if results could not be reliably repeated, or if the physical laws were prone to sudden alterations. The God of the Bible, unlike the Greek gods, is not capricious. The pioneers of modern science understood this as guaranteeing the non-capriciousness of natural law, making the whole scientific enterprise possible.

Many modern anti-creationists charge that the notion of a miracle-working God (as in six-day fiat creation) would destroy this particular foundation of science. They use this argument to redefine science in such a way as to exclude a supernatural original creation by definition, a priori. But the founders of modern science (all creationists) did not see it this way. They understood that there was no contradiction between the general uniformity of "natural law" (God's normative activity in upholding and sustaining the creation) and the miracles He is recorded as performing in the Bible. Since He is himself responsible for the lawfulness of His creation, He has the sovereign right to override it for His special purposes in one-off miracles, like raising the dead. The miracles of Scripture are not arbitrary exercises happening at a whim, likely to reoccur at frequent intervals. They are rare events of very special significance and purpose. They were instantly identifiable as miraculous, precisely because of the general principle of non-capriciousness in all things. (Generally, dead men don't rise, nor can live ones walk on water.)

In short, whatever benefits science has brought to the world (real science, not evolutionary/long-age storytelling) can be traced back to belief in the Bible, and in literal creation in particular. Even many secular scholars agree.

Economic Opportunity

If you looked at such a typical list of countries in which most would want their children brought up, there is a strong correlation with capitalism and the free enterprise system. So it is hardly surprising that many see the capitalist economy, per se, as the real key to desirable living.

With the collapse of the Iron Curtain and the demise of socialism/communism, it was assumed that all Russia had to do was to adopt a Western-style capitalist system in order to rapidly reach a new era of peace, prosperity, and personal freedom. Not many foresaw the catastrophic result, unaware that free enterprise thrives on "cultural morality." The notion of private property is repeatedly sanctioned and upheld in the Bible. ("Thou shalt not steal" only makes sense if an individual has private property capable of being stolen.) The virtuous woman of Proverbs 31, whose children "rise up and call her blessed," is clearly running a business. But the Bible puts all this in the context of a society underpinned by strict moral law. Dealing must be just, weights and measures must be precise, the poor are not to be oppressed, and so on — a moral law eternally decreed by the Creator and stamped on the human heart and conscience, as well as enforced by the authorities.

To work to the benefit of a society, the free enterprise system needs such a cultural backbone of agreed-upon morality. Despite the West increasingly turning its back on God, there is still an embedded substrate of this morality. After 70 years of official atheism, reinforced and sustained by a relentless program of indoctrination in evolution/long-ages, Russian society (which was not part of the Reformation's sphere of influence anyway) had little such foundation left. If everything just evolved, then there is nothing "out there" to act as an absolute standard of right and wrong. Public order depended on the harshness of the state, rather than an inherent social morality. Imposed upon such a foundation, capitalism led to chaos, in which the law of the Darwinian jungle reigned. The most ruthless robber barons and "mafia" types prospered astronomically, while most of the rest of the population was plunged into such misery that huge numbers yearned for the once unthinkable — a return to the days of communist certainty.

Compare this to the economic foundation that made America great, the Protestant/Puritan ethic, in which one worked hard (and honestly) in business as service to one's fellow man. The money was a secondary issue — though important, it all belonged to God anyway. It is obviously no coincidence that cultures that have this post-Reformation heritage are more likely to have strong economic systems. Countries and cultures which missed out on this heritage are generally riddled with corruption, which holds back true economic advance. The Philippines and Indonesia, for example, are blessed with enough natural riches, fertile soil, etc. to ensure a good standard of living. Yet endemic corruption caused a yawning disparity between the super-rich and the very poor majority. Many African nations, disenchanted with failed socialism, have tried to graft capitalism onto similarly dysfunctional cultures — without good results. The reasons are not racial, but involve the foundational world view of the culture.

Where Are the Visible Christians?

Our Western society still lives off the accumulated "capital" of its biblical heritage, but this is rapidly being depleted; virtually none of the people that influence our culture are rock-solid Bible-believing Christians. Our widely perceived social decline, even in the midst of material plenty, is the result. Why are the movers and shakers of society the least likely to be Christians? It is because they are among the chief beneficiaries of higher public education. Politicians, lawyers, judges, teachers, media moguls . . . they are the ones who have been the most relentlessly exposed to the teaching of evolution and millions of years as "fact." This teaching has, in effect, been telling them that "the Bible has been disproved by science." Since Christianity's foundational doctrines (concerning sin, death, and the whole reason for the gospel) are based on a literal Genesis, it has also been telling them that "Christianity is based on myths and fairy tales." (Meanwhile, most of the church has sat passively by, mesmerized by the mindless mantra that Genesis and science is "a divisive side issue.")

These influential folk, indoctrinated against a biblical world view, have spearheaded the rapid shift in our society's foundation, particularly over the last half of the 20th century, from one based on biblical creation to one based upon a man-centered lack of absolutes. By no means are all of them atheists; many still attend church. Former U.S. Vice President Al Gore was able to attend church services yet at the same time write a book in which he said we all evolved from the sea. This is, he said, the likely reason for the significance of the water of baptism.

Many millions of churchgoers think in such "split" ways, too, because they have been trained to see their Christianity as being in a separate "box" to the rest of reality. The church has mostly presented Christianity as if it were only real "in your head," i.e., having only to do with abstract things such as morality and salvation, but nothing to do with the real world of rocks, trees, fossils, etc. Jesus pointed out that if we didn't believe Him concerning earthly things, we would scarcely believe Him about heavenly issues (John 3:12). So it is not surprising that disbelief in the Bible's history of "earthly things" leads to a watering down of its teaching on things such as morality. Many of the laws which have so appalled many Christians regarding abortion and homosexuality, etc. were passed by professing Christian legislators, thoroughly "evolutionized" by the culture, yet still blithely attending conservative churches.

Lawlessness and Legalism

We would expect an increase in lawlessness from the extensive penetration of our culture's foundation by anti-biblical thought patterns in the guise of "science." No maker means no accountability. A shift away from the Bible as truth must lead to a general decline in concern for one's fellows, increased general selfishness and decreased respect for authority. Almost everywhere I lecture in the once-Christian West, people can recall a time when they would leave their keys in the ignition of their car while shopping, without much concern. In fact, the first Holdens (General Motors cars made in Australia) were made so that no key was needed to start them. Today, they and others like them come with multi-thousand-dollar immobilizer systems as standard security — and still get stolen in frustratingly large numbers.

Even our responses to lawlessness reflect this foundation-shift. While our laws and expectations still have many vestiges of our biblical heritage, there are frightening signs of rapid decline. In many parts of my country, Australia, businessmen still remember when they would routinely seal major deals with a handshake. Today, teams of lawyers are engaged to draw up 30-page documents to perform the same function. It's not just that decline in individual morality makes the legal complexities more necessary, but that despite verbose contracts, the "system," including going to court to enforce such agreements, is far less likely to lead to just outcomes.

The Bible teaches that "righteousness exalts a nation" in ways which extend God's "common grace" to even the unbeliever for the short time he is on earth. Obviously, the ways in which it does so include direct national blessing by God. But I think that there are also intrinsic socio-economic consequences for degrees of righteousness in a culture, somehow built into the way God's world works. Small business in the West is, overall, experiencing a nightmare increase in bureaucracy and red tape. As personal morality has declined, and people bend the rules more, governments try to compensate by issuing more and tighter rules. These increase in complexity until they threaten to strangle the very system they are trying to protect.

In other words, as the once-biblical moral base of Western society declines, so it becomes, ironically, more moralistic in all sorts of areas. A culture with a social consensus of implicitly agreed-upon moral absolutes and values could get by with less legislation, because one could rely to some extent on the "spirit" of laws, without having to plug every loophole, dot every "i" and cross every "t." ("Common sense" is what the man in the street calls it. Today he shakes his head, not understanding why there is so much lack of this common sense.) In an evolutionized culture, one may not presume any more on such an implicit consensus, hence even legislation with noble motives, such as protection of the weak, becomes bogged down with more and more legalism. The outcomes may be technically correct, but absurd to the point of outrage.

I recall a case in South Australia in which a businessman fired an employee who had transferred $1,800 from the employer's account into his own. The employer had to pay compensation for unfair dismissal, because it had not been clearly established by the employer that stealing was a just cause for dismissal. In any case, it had not been proved that the employee did not intend to return the funds. A small firm in New South Wales had to reinstate a mechanic they had dismissed for turning up to work drunk. According to an interpretation of the legislation's fine print, they should have warned him not to work while drunk!

I'm sure most readers will recall other similar episodes reflecting this pattern, for example, burglars successfully suing for damages after injuring themselves during housebreaking. Man's attempts to write his own rules, independent of the Maker's handbook, the Bible, repeatedly preview their ultimate end in paroxysms of foolishness that would have been unimaginable a few decades ago, when Christians "roamed the earth."

Are the Christians Hiding?

Actually, I believe that the problem is not so much that not enough Christians still roam the earth; there are still quite a number of us around. It is that we are no longer able to salt the culture to the extent we once used to (Matt. 5:13). This, too, relates to our society's shift away from a creation-based foundation.

I grew up in a non-Christian home, but my parents largely lived by the Christian ethic, as did most Australians in that early post-war time. It is not that there were massively more genuine, born-again Christians than now, but the Christian ethic had a hugely greater influence on society. Christians were often regarded as "wowsers" (moralistic killjoys). But they were, albeit often grudgingly, seen as somehow upholding a standard of right and wrong which was good and absolute, regardless of one's opinion. This was because most of that generation still vaguely believed in a Creator who therefore had the right to set such absolute rules.

Even the "baby boom" generation after them, my own, only really had evolution/long-ages "pushed" in tertiary education. Since then, each generation has been more and more thoroughly indoctrinated at ever younger ages. No wonder that they see right and wrong as just a matter of one's opinion, or what one can get away with, whereas my parents' generation believed it was always wrong to steal, regardless of one's opinion or circumstances. Though non-Christians, they would have been horrified at today's increasing regard of homosexual behavior as somehow normal and acceptable.

Today, people are only being logical, and consistent with their increasingly un-biblical foundation, when they ask, "Why shouldn't Adam marry Steve?" After all, it's just another opinion. And so the Christians, far from being seen as upholding some immutable standard of righteousness that transcends our feeble human opinion, are now actually seen as evil people, not standing for right, but for intolerance, forcing "their opinion" down another's throat.

Human Rights and Compassion

Not many people realize how many of the things we take for granted in our culture in terms of social compassion are really the consistent outcomes of the way in which our societies were once based upon the Bible. It was brought home to me (back when I used to practice medicine) through some of my patients from countries like Malta, Iran, and even parts of Greece, telling me what it was like in hospitals "back home." It was, they said, standard practice for the families of patients to have to bribe the hospital authorities in order to ensure that the patient was adequately fed. If the patient needed to have shots of a narcotic painkiller, then an amount approaching the "street value" of the drug would first need to be paid to the head nurse.

Our higher level of social compassion is not the outgrowth of some inevitable progressive enlightenment, or intrinsic to the Anglo-Saxon character, but largely results from the Bible. It came especially through the massive social transformations wrought by the gospel preaching of giants like John Wesley, George Whitefield, and Jonathan Edwards. The genuine revivals that swept England and America, and touched the continent, were so different from what is called "revival" today. I don't want to imply that anything involving lots of Christians would have been all sweetness bathed in warm, rosy light (we are all fallen sinners after all, though redeemed). The overall reality, though, is that millions surrendered their lives to Christ's loving mercy, acknowledging the affront of their sin-stained lives in the sight of a holy Creator God.

Like a spreading flame, this 18th century Great Awakening surged across entire countries. Many of the individuals thus transformed became the movers and shakers of their day. In England, a few of these converts to Christ became parliamentarians with names that still reverberate down to our time, such as Shaftesbury and Wilberforce. These two were the prime movers behind the abolition of slavery, directly motivated by their born-again Christianity.

Pre-revival England was a pretty horrible and heartless place, with children routinely being forced to labor in mines, and tortured if they resisted. The influence of the gospel on Western society affected not just the abolition of slavery and child labor, but prison reform, hospital reform, orphanage reform, and much more. This was not driven by emotion so much as by a robust Christian world view, based on a totally trustworthy and historically accurate Bible. Because it reached all levels of class and education, it also reached the lawmakers and other influential people. Today, it is the influential strata of society who, being the most "evolutionized," are most "immune" to gospel preaching.

Fortunately, the Great Awakening arrived before the views of Darwin (and the long-agers that preceded him) had captured the public mind and seduced the bulk of the Church into surrendering biblical authority. One can only shudder at the direction our world might have taken had it been otherwise. If the bulk of the population had believed then, as now, that science made nonsense of the Bible's history, would millions of them have believed its gospel message, so inextricably rooted in that history? Would they have repented in tears for their sin if they believed that sin was just some leftover collection of instincts from their animal ancestry? And where would that have left us in regard to slavery, and all of the social reforms and liberties held dear by even the most ardent humanist?

Women in Society

Part of the sinful tendency in humanity is for men to pervert their God-given authority role into a corrupt exploitation of the "weaker sex." History shows that nowhere has this been more minimized than in Bible-centered, gospel-transformed cultures. People were given, Genesis tells us, dominion over the rest of creation, but not over each other. There is no biblical justification for one person having dominion over or exploiting another (as opposed to being in an authority role, a different issue altogether). Paul says, in Galatians 3:28, that in Christ there is no male nor female, just as there is no Jew nor Greek, slave nor free — even though all these categories existed. His point is clear.

I recall being approached, after giving a sermon on Genesis, by a smiling but tight-lipped Salvation Army woman officer. She said that she believed Genesis 1, but not Genesis 2. Puzzled, I asked her to expand on that.

"Because in chapter 2 it says that Adam was created first," she said, "but in chapter 1 it teaches that they were both made together."

I told her that the language in Genesis 1 certainly taught nothing contrary to chapter 2, and that Adam's creation prior to Eve was actually reiterated in the New Testament (1 Tim. 2:13). But what was her real problem with who was created first? (I guess I had an inkling from knowing the verse before, 1 Timothy 2:12.)

"Because I don't think that men are more important than women," she explained.

"You know something?" I said. "I don't think they're more important either, and neither does the Bible teach that. Genesis 1:27 tells us that both men and women were made in God's image. But the Bible does teach different roles, such as headship in marriage, authority in the church, and so on, which doesn't mean that anyone is less important to God." Setting her face even more tightly, she turned and hurried away.

Human Rights

Today there is more emphasis on our "rights" than ever. The U.S. Declaration of Independence wisely indicated that whatever "human rights" we have are because they have been endowed to us by our Creator. If we are just evolved effervescences of nature, what possible basis can there be for any absolute "rights"? Our opinion? What if my perceived "right" infringes upon yours — does it not then simply boil down to which of us is "stronger" in our society?

Because the notion of rights is so tightly bound up with the fact of biblical creation, there is so much more freedom, and human rights are always better protected, in countries and cultures which once had a biblical, creation-based foundation. That is also why we need to be concerned about the rapid erosion of that foundation in our own culture — because it will be hard to avoid the whole notion of "rights" becoming perverted.

Already, we see that unborn human beings have lost their "human rights," by the untold millions. Many anti-abortion activists think the key to winning the battle is to persuade the majority that the fetus is human. They miss the point of what happens as a society's foundation becomes evolutionized away from biblical absolutes. Without a belief in an absolute yardstick of right and wrong, something "out there, bigger than all of us" which transcends human opinion, there is no immovable taboo against taking a human life, either. The abortion-rights leaders are largely ready to concede that the fetus is human, anyway. But so what? No one made us, no one owns us, so if the majority wants the right to take the life of an unborn human, it's okay.

Influential Princeton philosophy professor Peter Singer (an Australian export, I'm afraid) is renowned for taking his evolutionary beliefs to their consistent conclusion. Since Genesis is not true, he says, we know that people are not somehow special, made in God's image. Hence, they have no intrinsic "rights" over and above the animal kingdom. Rights are what we bestow upon them as a society.

Thus, their usefulness to society, or their "stage of humanness," or whatever other arbitrary criterion we choose, is just as good as any other to determine their right to life; there is no such absolute right.

Singer has said that at one stage in its development, the unborn human baby has no more "rights" than a lettuce, because even though both are biologically alive, neither has a functioning nervous system. Later, the developing embryo has more rights than a lettuce, but still less than a rabbit, and so on. (Singer is, not surprisingly, an ardent campaigner for the rights of animals. An intelligent ape would have, for him, more "right to life" than a severely retarded human being. It all makes sense on an evolutionary foundation of thinking.) But why should this process of gradual assignment of rights stop at birth? Horrifyingly, Singer has taken the next logical step and supported the idea of infanticide, that is, that society should adopt some time after birth (two months — three, perhaps?) before assigning legal "humanity" to any infant, to allow a decision as to whether that infant should be allowed to live. Based on the sorts of arguments we have seen for abortion, it is likely that the issue of the baby's "wanted" status would feature prominently.

Singer and others increasingly advocate a utilitarian standard for assessing the "rights" of the old, disabled, and so on. Why should an elderly demented person be allowed to burden society, if Genesis is not true? (Interestingly, despite his public advocacy of such notions, Singer cannot live consistently with the starkness of his own evolutionary beliefs. He spends heavily on special care for his own mother, an Alzheimer's victim.)

The current push for "euthanasia" has the same roots as the abortion holocaust; a culture that has shifted foundation away from biblical absolutes, especially the Genesis "specialness" of human life, will ultimately want to get rid of those it deems a burden. The argument typically commences with pleas for compassion, not wanting people to suffer unnecessarily. Doctors who treat the terminally ill know there are many ways to relieve suffering short of killing someone.

Knowing our sin nature, once euthanasia is accepted in any guise at all, the floodgates are open. Might not Grandpa, with a lingering, expensive-to-treat illness, feel especially depressed (and thus ask to be legally killed) if he knows that his "euthanasia" could make the difference between little Johnny going to college or not? If Grandma happens to have an estate worth millions, will there never be palms greased by families to ensure medical "cooperation"?

Indeed, why should it end there? Why wouldn't society make it compulsory to euthanasize those utilizing its resources who have no perceived usefulness to themselves or others? Those who think that such things belong to the horrors of the Nazi era —they couldn't happen here — might think again. The Nazi regime commenced with laws for compulsory sterilization of the feeble, the racially impure, and so on. This was part of the eugenics movement, spearheaded by Darwin's cousin, Francis Galton. Famed British anthropologist and evolutionist Sir Arthur Keith wrote that Hitler's whole motive was to consciously make Germany conform to evolution, in which the strong ruled and the weak were culled or blocked from reproductive success. My mother, a gentle soul if there ever was one, grew up in Nazi Germany. She saw party banners being carried with slogans such as "We are sorry we have sinned against natural selection." She saw the films, squarely based on evolutionary "science," which promoted and justified this "racial hygiene." It all began to make sense; in fact appeals to "compassion" were the reason that she and millions of other Germans accepted the emptying of entire hospital wards by compulsory euthanasia. The chronically mentally ill, and so on, were killed in gas chambers that were later adapted for other "unfit" human beings.

While this was happening, many scientists in pre-war America and other parts of the West waxed enthusiastic about Germany's "scientifically enlightened" laws. Several U.S. states, and other Western countries, passed similar "eugenic" laws, and thousands of Americans, Swedes, and others were sterilized against their will. It not only could happen, it did.

This evolutionary impetus shuddered to a halt at the end of World War II, when the revelation of the horrors of the Nazi death camps profoundly affected the world. Anything with the vaguest hint of Nazi overtones was suspect, and the "eugenics" movement was forced underground. Embarrassed evolutionists, seeing the full consequences of "applied evolution," beat a temporary retreat in the "culture wars," which I am convinced dramatically slowed the decline of the West for a decade or more.

There has since been a conspiracy of silence about the Nazi/evolution connection. I recall *Time* magazine pondering not long ago as to why so many scientists and medical doctors so willingly took part in the ghastly Nazi experiments of the time. But in giving the answer, the writer could only bring himself to use the phrase "applied biology" to describe the Nazis' motivation. The "e-word" was conspicuously absent, unlike references to evolution in the writings of Hitler and his henchmen.

Many Christian writers have dwelt long on all these social declines. My purpose is not to start another round of tut-tutting, or to inspire a retreat into pietistic gloom. I want to highlight the importance of understanding why these things have happened, of how our corporate apathy in the Church about the origins issue, especially misunderstanding the nature of the battle about biblical authority and science, has contributed so much to not only our own demise, but that of the secular portion of our nations as well. Hopefully, this will motivate many Christians to join this battle, working to restore the biblical foundations of our culture, beginning with the Church.

The bright spot in all this, if there is one, is that even the bulk of non-Christians recognize that there is "something wrong" with the way things are headed. It gives a tremendous opportunity to open conversations with them about why. Almost every day in our ministry we hear of people who have come to Christ because Christians who now understand "where the battle is at" use such materials as *Creation* magazine and other creation materials to share with them — not only about "the evidence," but about why people think the way they do, and why things are declining as they are.

Preaching and Changed Foundations

One might ask, if the great revivals of the past have done so much good (not just in souls saved, but social benefit, too), why not do the same — just preach the same gospel message? One should further ask, though — why aren't those who are preaching in this way seeing anything like the results as during the Great Awakening?

To help us understand, consider the visit to Australia by renowned American evangelist Billy Graham in the 1950s. One-quarter of Australia's population turned out to hear him preach. Today, that would be like having more than 50 million Americans, or 5 million Australians, attending one series of evangelistic meetings. It wouldn't happen, would it?

The message Graham gave was basically that which the apostle Peter gave in Acts chapter 2. The results were incredible, too. Crime statistics dropped noticeably across the nation. Despite many falling away subsequently, many tens of thousands went on to become strong, active believers. It is hard to move in evangelical circles in Australia today without still coming across people whose Christian life commenced with those 1950s meetings.

Why is it that most people agree that such things

would not happen today in any Western nation? It is, as we have pointed out over and over, because of the foundational shift in the culture caused by the incessant undermining of biblical authority via "science."

This was demonstrated when Graham returned to this country in the 1970s and preached the same message. By comparison, it was a dramatic flop, in both turnout and professed conversions. The gospel had not lost its power, but the audience had undergone this foundational shift in the intervening years. A "Peter" message suited to believing Jews, who accepted the Old Testament background without which the gospel makes no sense, was more suited to 1950s Australia. Most people then, including the unbelievers, did not see the Bible as a book that had been discredited by "science." There was a general tendency for non-Christian parents to respect the Bible, and even to send their children to Sunday school. So when the evangelist held up his Bible and thundered, "The Bible says . . ." it was not an object of derision as it is for most today. People generally knew what "sin" meant. But in the seventies, what did sin mean any more? People were more conscious than ever of the idea that fossils and dinosaurs preceded people by millions of years. But since fossils show death and bloodshed, the idea that Adam's rebellion changed a perfect world to one dominated by sin and death was shattered.

To make the point that it was not some change in the preacher or his message, around the same period in the seventies, Graham also went to Singapore, where the same message had a tremendous harvest, reminiscent of Australia in the fifties. Why the difference? Unlike Australia's two decades of "evolutionization," the education system in Singapore focused on the skills needed to survive economically on a small island of mostly cars and concrete. Biology, geology, and long-age speculation barely registered on their list of educational priorities — engineering, commerce, law, medicine, etc. were taught instead. Most graduates had only the vaguest idea of any alleged contradictions between the Bible and science. The "ground" into which the gospel seed was sown was thus not as hardened, not as choked by the rocks and weeds of evolutionary/long-age thinking, as in Australia.

We need to understand that people today are harder to reach. Paul was plowing harder ground when trying to reach Greeks rather than Jews, and he knew he had to adapt his message. He could not start in the same place as Peter did; he could not assume the same background knowledge and belief. Today the ground is harder still, because it is not just that people don't understand the big-picture issues of Genesis history without which the gospel makes no sense — it is also that they are trained to think that this Genesis history is wrong. Today, more than ever, we need to be prepared to give answers to defend our faith (1 Pet. 3:15). Just presenting it is no longer enough.

Whose Fault Is It, Anyway?

We need to stop seeing "the world" as solely at fault for all this decline. We, the Church, bear a large portion of the blame. Why do "they" have the ability to blare out the message of "millions of years is fact — the Bible tells lies," over and over? Why do they have control of society's "microphone"? Because we handed it to them! Because we — let's face it — were more concerned about the fear of man, afraid of ridicule or peer pressure, rather than the fear of God. Because we said, "that's not our battle," and made it seem as if the Bible was not concerned with real-world history. Because we stood by while they educated our children and grandchildren with "evidence" that was squarely (mis)interpreted in an anti-biblical framework. Because, anesthetized by foolish, un-biblical and unworkable compromises like the "gap" and "day-age" theories, we stood by and did nothing while generations of the best and brightest of our Christian young people went to higher education like sheep to the slaughter, completely unprepared to cope with the torrent of humanistic "science" that would befall them, even in most "Christian colleges." And we then wonder why, as a result of this "unnatural selection" process, there are so few Christians in positions of influence in our culture, the very opposite of what happened after the Great Awakening.

The Church has, by and large, not seen fit to devote its resources to the defense of the faith in this most crucial of areas, namely the issue of how the history given in the Bible stacks up against real-world facts. Our thinking has too often been inverted in its priorities. Instead of building our understanding of the real world upon the Bible, we try to understand the Bible in the light of some fallible, ephemeral interpretation of facts by fallen, fallible people (as we all are).

Or we give the impression that we can somehow "prove" the Bible with science, which gives science (particularly the type that studies one-off past events) a credibility and legitimacy that even most secular philosophers don't assign to it. And despite the best of intentions, we have therefore placed "science" in a position of authority over the Bible.

The Answers

The answer to our culture's decline still is true revival; the right sort of change to counter the wrong sort. But revival seems unlikely until and unless we rediscover and rethink, en masse, this whole issue of biblical authority applied to all areas of life, including science and learning. While at university, I was an evolutionist and atheist, but I had read much of the Bible. Perhaps naively, I thought that being a Christian was supposed to mean accepting what Jesus Christ taught and believed. It was clear to me that Jesus believed in a literal Genesis and a young world, with people present "from the beginning of the creation" (Mark 10:6) — not billions of years after the beginning, as most evangelical leaders believe. I was amazed that none of the Christians I came across accepted what I, as an unbeliever, could easily see that the Bible taught and Christ believed — a literal Genesis and a young world.

My fellow humanists and I had nothing but contempt for the ducking and weaving of those who were obviously not willing to believe their own book. Those of the "God said it, I believe it, the evidence is irrelevant" variety (i.e., those who had most thoroughly separated the Bible from reality) had no hope of reaching us, either.

We don't need any more strategies and gimmicks for attracting larger congregations. We need to see a repenting in tears for the huge compromises in which we have engaged for a century or more. We need to keep on researching and refining the issues within the framework of biblical history. And we need to be training armies of our young people in how to think from a biblical foundation, ensuring that they are able to logically understand and defend their faith and how it connects to the real world.

The Church in the West, by and large, effectively withdrew from the fray many decades ago. The subsequent "rot" has taken a long time to set in, and it will take a long time to undo, should the Lord tarry. Let us "occupy" till He comes (Luke 19:13), not with idle squabbles about lesser issues, nor wringing our hands in helpless frustration at the decline around us, but with fighting the really significant battles of our time. The exciting thing about this battle for biblical authority is that the more you spread the information around that the Bible is true and can be trusted, the more people give their lives to Christ in the process. In the "big picture," that's the only sort of change that counts.

Chapter 6

YE SHALL BE AS GODS

The Modern Search for Extraterrestrial Life

Jonathan Henry

R ural America. Quiet country roads. Hay rides with friends and family on Saturday night. Sunday afternoon. Family gatherings on wide, shady front porches. You left your front door open all day, your house unlocked all night. Safety. Security. Our grandparents' time.

One hundred years ago. Small town America. Saturday evening socials at the Quaker church — "Friends' Church," it was called. Community. Togetherness. Belonging. Sunday morning. Church bells chime through the neighborhood. Monday morning. Classes in the one-room schoolhouse where America's Christian heritage was taught and revered. Where Christmas was a cause for private worship and public celebration. Innocence and happiness.

One hundred years ago. The big city. New York. Streets so safe you could walk them at night. Evangelistic services on Saturday night — hundreds converted. Moody. Sankey. The great revivals. Bars closed. Crime down. God's kingdom coming closer every day.

These idyllic pictures of America were reality for

many. They endured through the late 1800s and into the early 20th century. Then came World War I.

World War I. Millions dead — the highest death toll of any war in history until then. Thousands maimed and killed by poison gas — the new weapon of mass destruction — a death so awful that poison gas in wartime has been outlawed ever since. During the waning months of war in 1918, a global flu pandemic kills more millions — one of the largest death tolls from disease in history.

After World War I, prosperity and "normalcy" return, only to be interrupted by the Great Depression.

Then came World War II with a staggering 50 million dead, many more than World War I, accompanied by atrocities so evil that even today they are incomprehensible.

Prosperity again followed World War II, only to be shattered in turn by the riots of the 1960s, and the drugs and the sex revolution of the early 1970s. In the late 1970s and early 1980s there was a nostalgic yearning for earlier times, happier times. "Happy Days" and Fonzie were the craze. But it was a nostalgia without the reality. Crime soared. Corruption skyrocketed. Materialism — the substitute for spiritual reality — held America in its grip.

America today. A nation adrift with no spiritual foundation. Sexual crime and perversion at record levels. Unrepentant corruption all the way to the highest levels of government. Locked and bolted doors and windows, even in small towns. Insecurity. Fear. Danger. A prayer for our children's safety. A prayer for their very lives — today.

What Went Wrong?

World War I was the first horrible omen that all was not right with our culture, or with Christianity. What had been developing behind the scenes, unnoticed by lay people and ignored by the churches? What had so suddenly changed the world from benignly good to darkly evil?

Of course, such changes do not really happen suddenly. They are preceded by years of quiet transition — like cancer. The cancer patient who suddenly finds he is in serious danger has had cancer for perhaps years, quietly destroying from within. Likewise, World War I did not just suddenly happen for no reason. World War I had causes. So did the sexual revolution. The drug revolution. Corruption in government. Teen rebellion.

The present does not happen by accident. Yet we think and act as if it does. We accept teen rebellion as normal, for instance. "My teenager has to struggle and adjust before maturing," we say. Yet this was not the norm somewhat more than 200 years ago in colonial America. "Functional illiteracy" did not exist among educated people, and the college-bound student likely as not needed a mastery of Greek and Latin simply to be admitted. Such students were trained to become the leaders of the new America. They were not recovering from the wasted years of a lost adolescence. They did not accept the subnormal as normal.

What in the last century has changed our country from a bastion of goodness to a den of corruption? What forces in churches have worked to make us accept the sub-normal as normal? Why do the "revivals" of today bring no widespread spiritual or cultural change, compared to the genuine revivals of a century ago?

The answer is satanic philosophies — evil philosophies that have permeated the entire world and even control the thoughts and decision-making processes of Christians, those who claim to be followers of Jesus Christ. One of these phi-losophies, the oldest one of all, is the one that promises, "Ye shall be as gods . . ." (Gen. 3:5; KJV). This philosophy is acted out when man believes and behaves as he wants, not as God commands. With man as his own god, there is law-lessness, and chaos, crime, and corruption result.

The 1800s was the century during which this philoso-phy reared its head in the West. It is well known that since the 1830s, evolutionism has dominated Western thought. A fact less recognized is that in the late 1800s, Hinduism was imported into the West under what came to be called the New Age movement. Though the term "New Age" is many decades old, it was not popular until the 1980s. If this seems surprising, we should remember that "the mystery of iniquity doth already work" (2 Thess. 2:7), and that evil plans and purposes may be in preparation for quite a while before being unleashed on an unsuspecting public.

Implicit in evolutionism is the possibility that man may be capable of evolving into godhood. In fact, "traditional" atheistic evolution, which professes no belief in God, is slowly giving way to pantheistic "New Age" evolution, in which all creatures are gods. It is also well known that godhood is the goal of the New Age movement.

As we shall see, this was Nimrod's philosophy at Babel, and it remains the philosophy of Oriental Hinduism, which dates back to the time when man dispersed to the East from Babel. In turn, the New Age is merely a form of Hinduism, "repackaged" for the Western mind. Both the New Age and Hinduism are extremely evolutionary, and the non-traditional evolutionism of these systems teaches that the "human animal" is becoming god. Indeed, the roots of modern evolutionism itself are found in Hinduism, as we trace back through Darwin, to the earlier skeptics, then to the Renaissance philosophers, and finally to Greece, the source of Renaissance rationalism. Greece borrowed evolutionary ideas from the East via Egypt.

It's All Happened Before

Genesis chapter 10 tells us about Nimrod, the builder of the Tower of Babel. This Tower was one of the great monuments of antiquity. By Nebuchadnezzar's time (about 600 B.C.), the Tower was some 2,000 years old. Nebuchadnezzar is reputed to have restored the Tower and, according to some archaeologists, mounted on it the Hanging Gardens of Babylon, one of the Seven Wonders of the ancient world.[1]

Genesis chapters 10 and 11 tell us much about Nimrod besides the fact that he was the driving force behind the Tower project. Genesis 10:10 states, for example, that Babel was merely "the beginning" of Nimrod's kingdom. Situated not too far from Babel were a number of other cities named in Genesis 10:10–12. Some of these cities, such as the ruins at Accad, have been unearthed by archaeologists. These excavations have revealed a fascinating pattern in the location of these cites. They appear to have been more or less equidistant from Babel, forming a ring of "satellite cities" around Babel itself.[2] The picture thus begins to emerge of Nimrod as a ruler masterminding the construction of a centralized city, Babel, flanked by a bloc of protective outposts or gulags.

This picture comes into clearer focus when we examine Genesis 10:9. This verse describes Nimrod as a "mighty hunter before the LORD." To be sure, Nimrod no doubt hunted and eliminated wild beasts and predators, thus establishing his reputation as a protector and leader. But the Hebrew wording in Genesis 10:9 carries a more sinister meaning which implies that Nimrod was doing more than hunting beasts. Nimrod was hunting men, presumably to force them into his growing empire.

Nimrod may have employed military force to support his drive for supreme control. However, Nimrod's actions were all done "before the Lord," which in the Hebrew signifies that Nimrod's actions were an offense to God. In modern slang we would say that Nimrod had an "in-your-face" attitude. In Genesis 9:1–3, God had instructed Noah and his descendants to "replenish," or fill, the earth with humankind. But contrary to God's command, Nimrod was working to coerce all people to stay near Babel. Leaving Nimrod's kingdom may have been as difficult as leaving the Soviet Union was a few years ago, and just as deadly.

With his empire shaping up, Nimrod set to work establishing a new religious system. What kind of religious system was this? Genesis 11:4, in describing the building of the Tower of Babel, tells us that the Tower was built "unto heaven." However, this phrase does not mean that the Tower literally reached the clouds.

The ruins of the Tower — or at least ruins thought possibly to remain from Nebuchadnezzar's restoration — are near modern Baghdad. From these and other similar ruins, archaeologists have estimated that the Tower was as high as several hundred feet. The Tower was therefore an imposing monument, but not high enough to pierce the clouds. The building of the Tower "unto heaven" literally means that it was built "unto the glory of the heavens." In the same sense we might say that a church building has been erected "unto the glory of God." In other words, the Tower was built to worship the heavens. This system survives as astrology, the false religion in which the stars and the planets are "worshiped" as sources of revelation. The constellations of astrology in fact are dated by secular historians as originating at the time biblical chronology indicates for the Tower itself.[3]

It is no coincidence that Nimrod is recognized as the father of astrology. But he was also the father of all systems of false religion which worship created things rather than the Creator (Rom. 1:25).[4] In particular, man began to worship himself as god, and to see in the heavenly bodies all sorts of overblown human attributes. This is why the pagan cultures of antiquity worshipped the sun, moon, and planets as supermen and superwomen. Man indeed had become god!

The ancient Jewish historian Josephus relates that Nimrod built the Tower of Babel on a foundation of lies. He told the people that the Tower would be their place of refuge if ever God sent another flood.[5] However, God had told Noah that He would never send another flood (Gen. 8:21). Furthermore, even as Nimrod was lying about God's care for His people, Nimrod was devising his nature-based religion to turn men away from God forever.

It is sobering to realize that Nimrod's attempt to establish control over mankind was stopped only by divine intervention. God himself acknowledged that no mere mortal could stop Nimrod's devices, for in Genesis 11:6 we read that God said, "Now nothing will be restrained from them, which they have imagined to do." God therefore interrupted Nimrod's plans by confusing the languages of mankind. Ever since, difficulties in communication have made global rebellion against God virtually impossible.

It's Happening Again

Satan, the creature ultimately behind Nimrod's plans, has a consuming desire to displace God. "I will be like the most High" (Isa. 14:14) has been Satan's cry of rebellion ever since he was cast from heaven and tempted Adam and Eve in the Garden of Eden. Since then Satan's desire to displace God has not changed, and neither have his tactics changed. He enticed Adam and Eve with the promise, "Ye shall be as gods." False religions from the cults to the New Age still make the same promise.

Satan's tactics in using Nimrod to struggle for world control have not changed either. It is no coincidence that Nimrod's empire has likenesses with the world system of today. We have seen that Nimrod was building his kingdom, his world system, "before the Lord." He did not care what God wanted. Nimrod's theme was "I did it my way." The world system today tells us, "Do your own thing. If it feels good, do it."

The world also tells us that we are not to be concerned about what God thinks. We should think and believe and act as we want. Man therefore tends to displace

God with the false gods of "self" and human opinion, false gods which can lead to other forms of false worship — and ultimately to the worship of man and the heavens as divine. Just as Nimrod led the people to worship the heavens, we are seeing a virtual worship of the heavens arising in our culture today. It is not merely that evolutionism and other false systems place human opinions ahead of what God says. The fact is that the New Age, Hinduism, and evolutionism are all promoting a single theme which, it is claimed, will lead man to higher development, and eventually to godhood. That theme is . . .

The Search for Extraterrestrial Life

As recently as 35 years ago, the existence of life in outer space was believed to be highly questionable, and many scientists regarded such an idea as flatly unscientific. Then in 1966 a best seller was published with the title *We Are Not Alone*.[6] The author wanted to believe in extraterrestrial life, but admitted that it might not ever be found.

In the last 20 years, however, a tremendous change in the attitude toward extraterrestrial life has shaken the scientific world. Noted astrophysicist Carl Sagan was perhaps the single most potent catalyst for this change. His "Cosmos" series,[7] which aired for several months in 1980 on the Public Broadcasting Service, forcefully insisted — backed up by stunning pictography and Sagan's persuasive way of speaking — that there was indeed extraterrestrial life. All scientists had to do was find it.

Now the Search for Extraterrestrial Intelligence (SETI) became fashionable. Scientists found that it was easy to get research grants to study extraterrestrial (ET) life. The existence of ET life was no longer questionable. It was a virtual certainty.

In the 1980s movies and headlines endlessly and dogmatically repeated the certainty that ET life was "out there." There was, of course, the movie *ET*, which grossed one of the largest box office takes in history. Even the scientific magazines and journals got into the act. In 1992, for example, the popular but serious magazine *Sky and Telescope* adorned its cover with large yellow print screaming, "NEW PLANETS DISCOVERED." After all, one has to have planets where the alleged ET life could live. And the artwork on the cover of this issue made the planets look exceedingly real.

The fanfare continued. If there are planets with other civilizations, then these planets must be organized into solar systems. Accordingly, the journal *Astronomy* for April 1996 announced in a feature article the existence of "Two New Solar Systems."

Meanwhile, the New Age movement was coming into its own. Shirley MacLaine, the high-priestess of the New Age movement, wrote the best-seller *Out On a Limb*,[8] in which she claimed that extraterrestrials had visited earth, and that untold numbers of people worldwide believed in extraterrestrial visits as absolute realities.

Where did Christian faith fit into all this? Shirley MacLaine and other "true believers" in ET life denounced Christians as dull-witted reactionaries who stupidly refused to see the truth about ET life. Some radical New Agers claimed that the Rapture would really be a snatching away of Christians by aliens. A few radicals went so far as to voice their wish that they could get rid of the Christians without waiting for the extraterrestrial invasion! Such sentiments were accompanied by a rising tide of Christian-bashing, as expressed by humanist John Dunphy: "The classroom must and will become an arena of conflict between the old and the new — the rotting corpse of Christianity, together with all its adjacent evils and misery, and the new faith of humanism."[9]

In all this confusion, one thing was very clear: SETI and the hope of finding ET life were part and parcel of the pagan New Age movement. Nevertheless, the persistent fact remained that not one substantiated observation of ET life had been made by anyone! Compared with the incessant and dogmatic media claims for the reality of ET life, the complete absence of any real evidence for it is nothing short of amazing. We will later come back to this startling fact, but now let's examine the roots of the New Age movement and why it so desperately wants to find ET life. In the process, we will see that, sadly, Christians who are not vigilant have been aligning themselves with the New Age position.

Back to Nimrod

Modern evolution is changing. Scientists are rejecting Darwinism — evolution by mutations assisted by natural selection — realizing that neither mutations nor natural selection can explain evolution. "Anti-Darwinians" are claiming that "design requires a designer." Biblical creationists rejoice at this trend, but the rejoicing is premature. For instance, Michael Behe, in his otherwise excellent anti-Darwinian book *Darwin's Black Box*, refuses to say who the Designer is.[10] This leaves the role of Designer an empty one, to be filled possibly by a New Age Hindu-type of "force."[11]

The New Age and Hinduism are in fact connected. The modern New Age was initiated by the Theosophical Society in the late 1800s. Through this movement "knowledge of Hinduism and Hindu influence has penetrated Western culture."[12] Hindu integration into the West was also a major part of the program at one of the world's first ecumenical conferences in 1893, the "World's Parliament of Religions." Hindus, other Eastern mystics, and many other faiths gathered to plan the building of a world religion. Significantly, Hinduism in turn traces back directly to Nimrod's evil system at Babel.[13]

Nowadays, more and more evolutionists, seeing the hopelessness of atheistic Darwinism, are converting to Hindu-style evolution, which has a designer "force," coexisting life forms (e.g., dinosaurs living with man), and intelligent (not primitive) ancient man, and which agrees with biblical creationists that data disagreeable to Darwinism have been suppressed.[14] Unwary Christians think of these positions as a return to biblical creation and as uniquely biblical, but they are not. Hinduism believes them all.[15] There is one belief unique to biblical creation, however. That is the teaching of "recent creation" and a young earth.[16]

Christian parents and educators need to teach the whole truth about biblical creation, including young age. Some Christians claim that the age of creation is irrelevant,[17] but without young age, we have a version of creation compatible with Hinduism.[18] Neither is it sufficient to teach merely "intelligent design" by an undefined "god" or "force." Biblical creation means teaching (1) that the "intelligent designer" is the God of the Bible, and (2) that the creation was recent. To teach less than this is to yield ground to the assertions of the New Age, thus leaving our children vulnerable to New Age claims.

Since the World's Parliament of Religions in 1893, the Hindu/New Age influence in Western culture has been growing. Hindu words like guru, karma, mantra, and nirvana have permeated popular culture.[19] Furthermore, there is a connection between this shift toward New Age Hinduism and the growing acceptance of ET life as real. The New Age is Western-style Hinduism, and Hinduism has always believed in ET life and visitations from outer space. Serious believers in ET life see in the "alien" life forms higher levels of godhood to which man may aspire, concepts also taught by the New Age and Hinduism.

This connection is not new. In the 1970s, for example, Erich von Daniken wrote *Chariots of the Gods?*, in which he proposed that the earth had experienced many visitations from space. He even claimed that the biblical prophet Ezekiel had seen, not heavenly beings as the Bible describes, but extraterrestrials coming to the earth in UFOs. His main "evidence" for these claims? Ancient documents venerated by Hindus and New Agers alike.[20] In fact, the founder of the New Age movement and first head of the Theosophical Society, Helena Blavatsky, obtained many of her ideas from the same Hindu documents revered by the New Age and modern Hinduism.[21]

Despite the antiquity of the Hindu belief in ET life, there is no more supporting evidence for it than there is for the modern belief. Belief in ET life is not based on scientific data, as we will now see. Yet empty as this belief is, it not harmless. Guided by his belief in ET life, modern man is searching for spiritual insight from the heavens, thereby repeating the events which transpired at the Tower of Babel.

Are There Other Planets in Other Solar Systems?

Astronomers have found no irrefutable evidence of planets outside the solar system. Neither do scientists know for certain of any planets around any stars except the sun. Though there appears to be no reason, scientifically or biblically, that planets could not exist outside the solar system, the present claims for such planets are based more on evolutionary theorizing than on real observations.

To many scientists who believe in evolution, life should be evolving in many places in the universe. They believe there should be other solar systems with inhabited planets. Sometimes this desire to find other planets and solar systems leads to misleading newspaper and magazine headlines. As we have seen, *Sky and Telescope*, for instance, published an issue with the cover story, "New Planets Discovered,"[22] and *Astronomy* magazine published an article entitled, "Two New Solar Systems."[23] Titles like these give the impression that astronomers have indeed made new planetary discoveries.

The question we must ask when we see such headlines is, What did the astronomers really observe? With current technology, it is impossible for astronomers to see planets outside the solar system directly. Because planets shine only by reflected light, any such planets would be far too dim to see. Stars and galaxies are the only directly observable objects outside the solar system.

Why Do some Astronomers Believe There Are Other Solar Systems?

Amazingly, claims of new planets do not come from truly observing any planets. These claims are based on observing stars with certain characteristics. Some astronomers then assume that these characteristics are signs of new planets. Most stars, for example, are members of close-knit star systems in which most of the stars are not easily visible because they are dim. Alpha-Centauri is one such system. Alpha-Centauri used to be thought of as a single star. Then Alpha-Centauri was found to have a companion star, making a "double" or "binary" star system. Eventually, astronomers discovered another star in the Alpha-Centauri system. Now we know that this system has at least three stars, but two of them are relatively dim.

In a system like Alpha-Centauri, the gravitational force of the dimmer stars tugs on the brighter one, making it "wobble." The stellar companions of Alpha-Centauri were suspected to exist long before they could be seen, because astronomers could see the wobbling motion of Alpha-Centauri. Observations of the dim companions were not made until later, but astronomers have now carefully studied these dim companions and have found them to be stars, not planets.

Since most stars are in star systems, most stars wobble, being pulled by unseen stars too dim to observe. If the unseen companions orbit a star preferably (but not necessarily) somewhat like the sun, astronomers sometimes assume that the dim companions must be planets in a kind of solar system. This was the case in the *Sky and Telescope* and *Astronomy* articles mentioned earlier. Both of these articles acknowledged that the alleged planets might be dim stars. *Sky and Telescope* even acknowledged that all previous claims of new planets had been "debunked," including the earlier "New Planets Discovered" headline.[24]

A second property of some stars is that they are surrounded by clouds of gas. These stars are quite unstable and throw off gases explosively from time to time. Evolutionists sometimes think of such a gas cloud as evidence of a solar system in formation. According to this idea, our own solar system evolved over billions of years from a cloud of gas, so why should the same thing not be happening elsewhere?

Of course, our solar system did not evolve at all, and what's more, laboratory tests have confirmed that it's impossible for small particles of debris somehow to stick together and begin forming a planet. The real meaning of the debris surrounding some stars is that the cosmos is self-destructing. It is dying, because it is all "groaning" under the curse of sin (Rom. 8:20–22).

A Closer Examination of Specific "Planet" Claims

In science, it is possible to confuse belief in what we want to see with direct observation. Evolutionists are prone to this error. Evolutionary scientists want to verify their faith in evolving extraterrestrial life over all the cosmos, and to them there must be planets harboring this life. To them, their faith in the existence of extra-solar planets is a virtual observation. With regard to science, however, the question is, have any extra-solar planets been directly observed or not? Presently the answer is no. Many "scientific observations" set forth as proven facts in the media are nothing more than ideas which the evolutionary scientist wishes he could observe today and hopes he will observe tomorrow. This is the current state of secular theorizing about extra-solar planets. Ironically, the article from *Astronomy* magazine[25] verifies this very statement, though it purports to prove the opposite.

On page 50 of this article, we read, "In 1992, astronomers discovered the first planetary system beyond our own." However, 1992 was by no means the first time a planet or extra-solar system discovery had been claimed, only to be discredited later. The 1992 "discovery," first reported in 1991 in the English journal *Nature*,[26] was only one more claim in a long line of earlier failed claims. Concerning these earlier "discoveries," the comment has been made, "Over the years, Barnard's star, 61 Cygni, VB8B, and several other stars showed wobbles that were heralded as planet-caused. Each planet report was later debunked."[27]

Will such a debunking be the fate of the current "discoveries"? Even now there is no consensus on the planetary status of the 1992 "discovery": "Variation in the light signal was later embarrassingly shown to be caused by the earth's own orbital motion instead of by a new planet."[28] In view of the failed planetary status of the 1992 object, why did *Astronomy* magazine tout it as the "first planetary system beyond our own"? Evolutionary wishful thinking?

Significantly, one more failed "discovery" is mentioned in the "*Astronomy* article on page 55, an "object orbiting the dwarf star HD 114762 . . . discovered a decade ago." Initially hailed as a new planet, the object was found to have a surface temperature of approximately 2,000°C (3,600°F), making it too hot for a planet, but about right for a star. The *Astronomy* article describes it as "a low-mass star masquerading as a planet" (page 55). Thus, the dwarf star HD 114762 turned out to have a stellar companion, making it one of the majority of stars which is bound to other nearby stars in its own star system.

After the 1992 "discovery," the *Astronomy* article mentions only three other purported "planets": one near 51 Pegasi (discovered in 1995), then one near 70 Virginis, and another near 47 Ursae Majoris (these last two being the "solar systems" in the title of the article). On closer examination, these newer claims were not so solid after all.

On page 50, the "planet" near 51 Pegasi is described in misleading terms as "a Jupiter-mass world orbiting at only 1/100 the Jupiter-Sun distance." This object was first described in 1995.[29] It is actually 22 times closer to its star than the earth is to the sun. As a result, the surface temperature of this object probably exceeds 1,300°C (2,400°F), making it a low-temperature star, not a planet. Even the *Astronomy* article admits that "astronomers wonder if it has any relationship to the planets in our solar system" (page 50).

The object near 70 Virginis appears to be much heavier than the earth, yet is twice as close to its star as the earth is to the sun.[30] This object was publicized as having liquid water, a requirement for life,[31] but this was only speculation. Hailed as the Goldilocks planet because its temperature was "just right" for liquid water, the *Astronomy* article nonetheless admits that it is "probably a lifeless ball of gas . . . a stormy, violent world with winds that top 300 miles per hour" (page 51). Having eight times the mass of Jupiter, some astronomers say it is not a planet at all.[32] It may be a brown dwarf, a burned-out star now too dim to shine but retaining some of the primordial heat imparted to it during the creation week. The *Astronomy* article admits that "its large mass and eccentric orbit have fueled speculation that it might be a 'failed star,' known as a brown dwarf, rather than a planet" (page 55).

Finally, the object near 47 Ursa Majoris is 1,000 times heavier than earth and is twice the distance from its star as the earth is from the sun, resulting in a temperature of -100 degrees celsius (-150°F).[33] Like the object near 70 Virginis, it seems to be a burned-out star.

None of these objects has actually been seen, only inferred from the wobbling of the visible stars 51 Pegasi, 70 Virginis, and 47 Ursa Majoris. The *Astronomy* article acknowledges, "Astronomers don't know much about the planets because they don't yet have the capability to take pictures of them" (page 53). It is nothing more than speculation that the objects tugging on these stars are planets at all. Nothing is known about their diameters, chemical composition, or surface features (if any), and the evidence indicates that they are dim or burned-out stars. The *Astronomy* article repeatedly admits, "Astronomers know virtually nothing about the new planets" (page 52).

Despite the extremely dubious claim to planetary status of objects like the one orbiting 51 Pegasi, this object continues to be touted as one of the first and more certain proofs of planets outside the solar system.[34] Taken at face value, this would imply that earlier claims have been discredited. But even more to the point, if the object near 51 Pegasi is supposed to be one of the best evidences for such planets, how certain are the other claims constantly being publicized? Evidently, not very certain at all.

In other words, planets have been inferred to exist, but inference is not observation. Inference can lead to research which produces direct observation, but until that time comes, the inference is not hard scientific data. It may be only wishful thinking. Today much inference is motivated by anti-biblical assumptions, and these anti-biblical roots should prompt the Christian to be skeptical of such conclusions. For example, the inference of extra-solar planets is motivated by the hope of finding extraterrestrial life other than God and the angels. The *Astronomy* article continuously speculates on this possibility. In the quotations below, the speculative words are emphasized:

> "how prevalent life *might* be in the universe" (page 50);
> "*might* be just right to support life" (page 51);
> on Goldilocks, "the building blocks of life *could* form" (page 52);
> "it's *conceivable* they have moons with atmospheres . . . making life possible" (page 52);

> "it's *possible* that one or both systems have . . .
>   Earth-sized planets in Earth-like orbits"
>   (page 53);
> "*could* have terrestrial planets lurking in the
>   shadows" (page 53);
> "*suggests* . . . many . . . planets (page 53).

Evolutionists are grasping at straws to reach the conclusion that there could be life in such places. But then, the wish for extra-solar planets is part of a larger scenario built around the struggle of fallen man to avoid God at all costs — including the cost of sacrificing the body of scientific data on the altar of evolutionary speculation. Scientific data can lead men to Christ — "For the invisible things of him through the creation . . . are clearly seen" (Rom. 1:20)"— while evolutionary speculation leads people away from God and can lead one to a rejection of Christ, spiritual death, damnation, and hell.

In contrast to worldly thinking, the Bible teaches that "we have a high priest who can be touched with the feeling of our infirmities" (paraphrasing Hebrews 4:15). The Christian's high priest is not a fearful alien. Those involved in the "Search for Extraterrestrial Intelligence" (SETI) have a schizophrenic desire to find extraterrestrial life even while they are fearful of what the aliens might do once they are found.

The Christian therefore must avoid the "Star Trek" mentality of being enamored with imaginary alien life forms and planets which could harbor them. The Christian is to focus his thoughts, time, and fellowship on the real high priest of the creation, with the purpose of glorifying Him. To accomplish this purpose, we must be "bringing into captivity every thought to the obedience of Christ" (2 Cor. 10:5). In the sciences, this means we must examine the inferences and data generated by the secular community, "hold fast that which is good" (1 Thess. 5:21), and use legitimate observations to point to the Bible as the only valid source of spiritual truth.

We may need to minimize the world's goals and desires (e.g., the goal of SETI; the wish to find extraterrestrial life) in order to maximize Jesus' command to find abundant life in Him. Certainly, creationists should be teaching that "He must increase, but I must decrease" (John 3:30). To the extent that we magnify the ideas and opinions of fallen man, He decreases in our lives and in the lives of those we touch. He is exalted as we teach what His Word sets forth as the purposes for the earth, the planets, and stars, the cosmos, and for life itself.

As the world approaches the end of the age, we can be sure of one thing: claims for the reality of ET life and places where it lives will grow ever more dogmatic and convincing. The April 1996 *Astronomy* article we have examined is typical of these claims, and shows the uncertainty of them all.

Is There Extraterrestrial Life?

According to much of the media, ET life thrives in outer space. Some scientists used to think that ET life might exist on the moon. The Apollo 11 astronauts were even kept in quarantine for a time after returning to earth because of the fear they might have been infected by harmful lunar microbes. This was discontinued in later lunar missions because scientists came to realize that the moon is absolutely lifeless.

Some astronomers have proposed that strange forms of life might exist on other moons, such as Io and Europa (moons of Jupiter), or Saturn's moon Titan. However, there is absolutely no evidence of any life on these moons. Astronomers have found no evidence of ET life anywhere.[35] Nevertheless, some scientists have coined the term "exobiology" to refer to the study of extraterrestrial life. Theodosius Dobzhansky, the late evolutionist known worldwide in academic circles, has noted that exobiology is the only scientific discipline whose "subject matter has never been observed and may not exist."[36]

Despite the popularity of SETI, the Bible makes no mention of any life living outside the earth except God and the angels. This is significant, because the Bible was not written to apply only to the earth. The Bible applies universally. Genesis chapter 1, for example, makes sweeping statements of purpose for the heavenly bodies which apply to all places in the cosmos (Gen. 1:14–18), not just to the sun or the moon.

What are these purposes revealed in Genesis 1:14–18? The heavenly bodies are to provide light and serve as time-tellers by marking off intervals of time — seasons, days, and years — for the earth's life. How are we to respond to this fact? As Creator, God has the right to tell us why He made the heavenly bodies, and we have the responsibility to accept what He says as sufficient. We do not have the right to insist that God must have or should have created the stars to support life of their own. Neither do we have the right to insist that the stars must have spiritual purposes the Creator has not revealed to us. This is the error of astrology, the pseudo-science which insists that stars must have purposes outside the ones revealed by the Creator.

What Is Life?

Real life is not only physical, but spiritual. Amazingly, the author of all life would be dead according to the standard biological definition of life, for He does not change, metabolize, grow, or reproduce. This contradiction, that God, the most abundantly living of all beings, would be dead according to the definition of biology, demonstrates that "life" is not really equivalent with being biologically viable.

A system may be biologically viable and yet may not be truly "living" in the biblical sense. Many entities included in biology do not have the "breath of life" mentioned in Genesis chapter 1 which an organism must possess to be "living." Loosely speaking, the "breath of life" corresponds to the soul and spirit. Entities such as viruses, bacteria, or even plants are thus arguably not genuinely alive, though they are classed as biological organisms. There's food for thought here — maybe the scope of biology should be redefined. Maybe botany should be thought of as a physical science!

While it is hardly likely that the domain of botany will be redefined, what this means for the search for ET life is that the search cannot be confined to the detection merely of viruses or bacteria (though even these have not been found anywhere except earth). SETI must ultimately involve a search for spiritual life. Hebrews 4:15 tells us about genuine "ET life," our Creator God who is the author of all life. This verse tells us that He is not a fearful alien. He can "be touched with the feeling of our infirmities." We are not alone.

As a matter of fact, many evolutionary scientists have come to the realization that SETI is really a search for *spiritual* intelligence.[37] However, instead of searching for extraterrestrial intelligence, each of us must find spiritual life in the Lord Jesus Christ. Each of us must trust Him alone for personal salvation. Those who have trusted Christ alone can anticipate an eternity with Him, a future far more wonderful than the most imaginative science fiction.

What Is the Future for the Redeemed?

Revelation chapters 21 and 22 describe the future of those who know the Lord Jesus Christ as personal Savior. The redeemed will live in the New Jerusalem, going in and out without hindrance or physical constraint. The laws of gravity and inertia will no longer apply to the redeemed, for their bodies will be like Christ's glorified resurrection body (Phil. 3:20–21).

Furthermore, the New Jerusalem will be the focal point of the new heaven and the new earth. With bodies unconstrained by gravity or inertia, the redeemed will be able to explore the new heavens to an extent that science fiction writers cannot even begin to imagine.

All of this wonderful activity will be only for the glory of God, for there will be no sin in the new creation. There will be no cosmic evolution, astrology, or other false philosophy opposing the truth. All the products of sin — tiredness, sorrow, decay, and death — will be gone forever. This is why we can say that by trusting Christ alone for salvation in this life, the redeemed have a future life that makes the most imaginative science fiction seem as nothing by comparison.

What Are UFOs?

UFO stands for "unidentified flying object." Most UFO's are nothing mysterious at all. Many UFO sightings turn out to be clouds, ordinary planes, weather balloons, or artificial satellites high in the sky which have been misidentified as something strange.

Of the small remaining number of UFO sightings, most of them probably involve military technology not yet made known to the public. Flight tests of this technology seem strange and unfamiliar to anyone who happens to see it from a distance. The stealth technology developed to shield military aircraft from radar detection has been tested since at least the 1950s, but was not shown to the public until the 1980s. For many years, some people who thought they were seeing flying saucers from outer space were possibly seeing stealth aircraft being tested in flight. One Air Force officer has reportedly claimed that the military has technology that is "so far beyond the comprehension" of the average person as to seem "alien."[38]

The military base called "Area 51" in Nevada is well known among UFO enthusiasts as a site of alleged UFO activity. In fact, Area 51 is nothing more than a launching and storage base for advanced military aircraft, some of which may involve technologies still classified.

Finally, there is the possibility of demonic influence in some UFO phenomena. Many possible associations of UFO sightings with demonism and spiritism have been documented.[39] How can we put this possibility in perspective?

Astronomy has been an especially fertile ground for satanic deception. Cosmic evolution and astrology trap many people in systems of belief which prevent them from ever coming to Christ for salvation. An obsession with UFOs is simply one more possible trap. For many people, the widespread belief in extraterrestrial intelligence and UFO intelligence may be another way of avoiding their personal accountability to God. For an example, the so-called "Roswell incident" of 1947, in which extraterrestrial beings allegedly landed near Roswell, New Mexico, has become an obsession for perhaps millions of people.

Whatever happened at Roswell, the Roswell incident has convinced many people that wisdom and intelligence are to be found, not in God's Word, but somewhere out in space. Satan, the god of this world, is pleased to use any tactic that will keep a person from looking to the God of creation for true salvation and intelligence.

Furthermore, like SETI and the belief in ET life, UFOs feed into the belief system of the New Age and Hinduism, with "alien abductions" being characterized as "out of body experiences" and reincarnation, both of which are central tenets of these pagan systems.

Modern Man's Spiritual Hunger

The New Age and Hinduism are two very popular efforts of fallen man to find God. The ultimate motivation for SETI is also a quest for spiritual satisfaction apart from the true God. Thus, the New Age, Hinduism, and SETI are all compatible and reinforce each other in their message to modern man. That message is very clear: There are other ways to God and salvation than the gospel of Christ. The Bible is obsolete!

However, we have seen that it is really the claims of SETI that are bankrupt. Even more, the spiritual quest of SETI researchers comes through very clearly in what they say, revealing that the alleged "scientific" basis for ET life is often nothing more than a cover-up for spiritual concerns. As one writer has said, "The rationale for SETI is straightforward, yet awesome: If life exists elsewhere . . . in the Milky Way galaxy, and if other civilizations have arisen on distant planets, they may have been broadcasting radio messages to call attention to their presence. The earth has the means to receive these messages, in the form of giant radio telescopes being used for astronomy, and for communicating with spacecraft. By enlisting them in a systematic listening program, man may finally be able to answer those age-old questions: Is anyone out there? Are we alone in the universe?"[40]

The attitude expressed by this writer is one of rejecting the Bible with a vengeance, for the Word of God answered these "age-old" questions thousands of years ago. Yet modern man without God has little choice but to evolve into godhood himself. As we have seen, man evolving into a god is a central tenet of the New Age and Hinduism. Even more, man becoming god is the ultimate goal of both evolutionism and SETI. Not surprisingly, evolutionism and SETI are tightly intertwined, with each belief serving as a rationale for the other. If man has evolved, alien races must have evolved, too. And if other races have evolved, maybe they can show us our future: "It would be encouraging, SETI scientists say, to learn that other races survived the perils of nuclear technology, genetic engineering, and pollution, and continued to progress. Knowledge of very advanced races might give mankind a clue to the future of its own evolution."[41]

In the final analysis, SETI and the belief in extraterrestrial life are vital beliefs of the false systems of evolutionism, the New Age, and Hinduism, and these systems are exploding in the West as Western culture moves away from biblical foundations into a modern paganism. Christians must not confuse claims for ET life with "science." Since the Creator has told us why He made the heavenly bodies, Christians must also be careful not to impose on Him the idea that He must have made the universe to support ET life forms. In supporting the false messages of the world system, Christians would be buttressing — unintentionally or not — the belief that man's opinions are higher than God's thoughts. Man thus becomes his own god!

Christians must be faithful in proclaiming the biblical message that revealed truth is to be found only in God's Word and that salvation is to be found only in Christ alone. As we move toward the end of the age, the Christian message — both evangelistically and scientifically — should diverge ever further from that of the world, since the world will be moving ever further from the Bible. The Christian dare not frame a "new" message that accommodates the world's increasingly anti-biblical ecumenical and "scientific" claims.

Billions of people in the false systems of evolutionism, the New Age, and Hinduism are on spiritual journeys doomed to end in eternal disaster. Yet the Bible tells us that those who have come to Jesus Christ alone for personal salvation can have wisdom and intelligence simply by asking Him for it (James 1:5). Why should we search anywhere else?

Notes

1 C.W. Ceram, *Gods, Graves, and Scholars* (New York, NY: Vintage Books, 1986), p. 326–321.

2 H.M. Morris, *The Genesis Record* (Green Forest, AR: Master Books, 1976), p. 252–253.

3 J. Jeans, *The Story of Physical Science* (Cambridge University, 1951), p. 8: "The earth wobbles as it rotates . . . so that the portion of the sky

which can be seen from any portion of the earth's surface is continually changing; that part in which the constellations bear ancient names is the part which could be seen from about latitude 40° N, in about the year 2750 B.C., and this is thought to suggest that these constellations were grouped and named by the Babylonians of some such date. They are practically identical with our present-day constellations of the northern sky."

4   A. Hislop, *The Two Babylons* (New York, NY: Loizeaux, 1959; reprint of 1916 edition), p. 14–19, 289–290.
     R.E. Woodrow, *Babylon Mystery Religion* (Riverside, CA: Ralph Woodrow Evangelistic Association, 1993), p. 1–6.

5   F. Josephus, *Antiquities of the Jews* in *Josephus: Complete Works* (Grand Rapids, MI: Kregel, 1976); written about A.D. 100 and translated by William Whiston in 1737. Josephus writes (p. 30): "Now it was Nimrod who excited [the people] to . . . contempt of God. . . . He also gradually changed the government into tyranny — seeing no other way of turning men from the fear of God, but to bring them into a constant dependence upon his power. He also said he would be revenged on God, if he [God] should have a mind to drown the world again; for that he [Nimrod] would build a tower too high for the waters to be able to reach! and that he would avenge himself on God for destroying their forefathers!"

6   Walter Sullivan, *We Are Not Alone* (New York, NY: New American Library, 1966), p. 37, 172, 284.

7   The PBS "Cosmos" series was put into a book by Carl Sagan (*Cosmos*, New York, NY, Random House, 1980). Sagan was an atheistic evolutionist who denied the existence of the supernatural in statements such as the following: "The neurochemistry of the brain is astonishingly busy, the circuitry of a machine more wonderful than any devised by humans. But there is no evidence that its functioning is due to anything more than the . . . neural connections that build an elegant architecture of consciousness" (p. 278). As one who denied the supernatural, Sagan condemned metaphysical beliefs in ET life and UFOs, but he believed that many physical life forms inhabit the universe.

     Sagan also publicized the connection between Hinduism and cosmic evolution in the "Cosmos" series, which showed "a close comparison . . . between Hindu beliefs and concepts of the Big Bang" (J.K. Beatty, "Carl Sagan's 'Cosmos': Prime-Time Astronomy," *Sky and Telescope*, vol. 60, no. 3, September 1980, p. 194).

8   Shirley MacLaine, *Out on a Limb* (New York, NY: Bantam, 1984), p. 308–309, 352–354.

9   J.J. Dunphy, "A Religion for a New Age," *The Humanist*, vol. 43, no. 1, January/February 1983, p. 28. Others have voiced similar sentiments: "Christianity has fought, still fights, and will fight science to the desperate end over evolution, because evolution destroys utterly and finally the very reason Jesus' earthly life was supposedly made necessary. Destroy Adam and Eve and the original sin, and in the rubble you will find the sorry remains of the son of God. . . . If Jesus was not the redeemer who died for our sins, and this is what evolution means, then Christianity is nothing" (G.R. Bozarth, "The Meaning of Evolution," *American Atheist*, September 1978, Vol. 20, p. 30).

10 M. Behe, *Darwin's Black Box* (New York, NY: Free Press, 1996). Behe states on p. 196: "Inferences to design do not require that we have a candidate for the role of designer." On the next page, Behe says again, "The conclusion that something was designed can be made quite independently of knowledge of the designer. . . . The inference to design can be held with all the firmness that is possible in this world, without knowing anything about the designer."

While such statements contain an element of truth, biblical creation requires that we affirm with the apostle John that the God of the Bible is the designer (John 1:1–3). Behe elsewhere claims that belief in a designer does not require any other belief consistent with biblical creation, such as recent creation: "The belief that the designer had to have made life recently . . . *is not a part of intelligent-design theory*" [emphasis his] (p. 227). There is a linkage between evolution with a non-God designer, and the belief in ET life. Commentator Marvin Olasky has observed, "The movement among some to replace the evolutionary paradigm with a belief in 'intelligent design' does not necessarily mean an increase in belief in God. One new line of defense for materialists is that the designer of life on earth came from a more advanced planet in another star system" (M. Olasky, "Outside the Beltway," *World*, vol. 11, October 12, 1996, p. 30). Ironically, in this same issue of *World*, on page 5, is an article praising Behe entitled "You Just Have to Sing." Christians can be thankful for the good things Behe says, but it seems that in the long view of history, considering the spread of paganism in the last century, there would be a need for caution in assessing Behe's position.

11 In addition to Behe's book, other authors have written anti-Darwinian books in recent decades. A sampling includes Michael Denton, *Evolution: A Theory in Crisis* (Bethesda, MD: Adler & Adler, 1985); William R. Fix, *The Bone Peddlers: Selling Evolution* (New York, NY: Macmillan, 1984); and Michael A. Cremo and Richard L. Thompson, *Forbidden Archeology* (San Diego, CA: Bhaktivedanta Institute, 1993). These authors span a wide spectrum of religious beliefs. Behe is a Catholic, Denton is an agnostic, Fix is a pantheist, and Cremo and Thompson are converts to Hinduism. All of them say that Darwinism is wrong, but none of them give credit to the true God for designing His creation. Henry Morris, president emeritus of the Institute for Creation Research in San Diego, has warned that intelligent-design theory without a return to God is *not* biblical creation. (H.M. Morris, "Neocreationism," *Acts & Facts*, February 1998, p. 1–4).

12 C.S. Braden, "Theosophy," Grolier Encyclopedia, Grolier, 1970, Vol. 18, p. 80. See also J.O. Fuller, *Blavatsky and Her Teachers* (East-West Publications, 1988), p. 44–45. The dust jacket of this book notes significantly that "Blavatsky's main work *The Secret Doctrine* (1888) . . . offered a profound spiritual interpretation of evolution, in contrast to Darwinism, and brought a new dimension into western thought." Blavatsky, not surprisingly, would thus appear to have been the first to propose "New Age" evolution.

13 J.H. Barrows, editor, *Proceedings of the World's Parliament of Religions* (Chicago, IL: Parliament Publishing, 1893), p. 6–8, 18, 38, 57, 74, 158. This conference was held in conjunction with the 1893 Chicago World's Fair. Some 10,000 letters of invitation and 40,000 documents were mailed

worldwide in preparation for this conference (p. 44), and more than 7,000 attended the closing session (p. 157). The ecumenical forces behind this conference are still active, and a centenary conference was held in Chicago in 1993. The ecumenical goals of the 1893 conference, however, have progressed so far that now virtually every major religious group embraces them, and the 1993 conference was not so much a huge working session as a commemoration of the 1893 conference.

The ultimate goal of ecumenism has never been merely the unification of Western religions, but the gathering of all faiths into a globalistic Hindu-style world church. This is evident from the *Proceedings* referenced above (p. 78, 87, 96, 192–193, 331, 456–457). It is in this light that we must understand the Pope's recent universalist claims that people of all faiths, including Hinduism, can be saved apart from Christ (A. Dager, "New Gospel Emerging," *Media Spotlight*, October 1997, p. 24). The pope and other ecclesiastical leaders are increasingly making such statements as Hinduism is "mainstreamed" into the ecumenical movement. Furthermore, New Age evolution is only one aspect of the emerging global religion, along with other components such as radical environmentalism and earth worship.

The connection of environmentalism and earth worship with Hindu-style paganism is discussed in M. Coffman and B. Alexander, "Eco-Religion and Cultural Change," *Spiritual Counterfeits Project Journal*, vol. 17, no. 3, July–September 1992, p. 15–23. The roots of Hinduism at Babel are documented in A. Hislop, *The Two Babylons*, p. 14–16, 19–20.

14   Geologist Virginia Steen-McIntyre, in a letter to Michael A. Cremo (the Hindu co-author of *Forbidden Archaeology* mentioned in Note 11): "Somewhere down the line the god of the Vedas [Hinduism] and the God of the Bible will clash . . . but until then the servants of both can agree on one thing — human evolution [Darwinism] is for the birds," in M.A. Cremo, *Forbidden Archeology's Impact* (Badger, CA: Torchlight Pub., 1998), p. 32.

15   Hindu beliefs about origins often sound like biblical creation, as Cremo notes in *Forbidden Archeology's Impact*: (1) On the coexistence of life-forms: "What we see is a pattern of co-existence, rather than evolution . . . just as today we see that human beings of various levels of civilization and culture co-exist with apes and monkeys" (p. 463); (2) On the high intelligence of ancient man: "If you were to predict what archaeologists might find . . . they would tend to find a . . . mixture of anatomically modern human fossils . . . crude stone tools [and] articles indicative of a higher level of culture (p. 464–465); (3) On the suppression of data disagreeable to Darwinism: "Orthodox scientists have often employed silence as the most effective way of responding to evidence that challenges an established doctrine" (p. 51).

An end sheet in *Forbidden Archeology's Impact* which advertises another book published by the Bhaktivedanta Institute says, "It documents hundreds of anomalies found in the archeological record that contradict the prevailing theory and shows how this massive amount of evidence was systematically 'filtered' out. . . . You can then judge for yourself how objective the scientific community is in its pursuit of knowledge!"

Biblical creationists would find much to agree with here. Yet Cremo says of himself that "I am an agent of Gaudiya Vaishnavism [a large Hindu sect with centers worldwide] . . . with an assigned project of [challenging] some fundamental concepts of Western science" (p. 22–23). Later he reveals that *"Forbidden Archeology* is designed to demolish the case for [conventional] biological and cultural evolution and to advance the cause of a Vedic alternative" [New Age evolution] (p. 122).

16 Hinduism believes in billions of years (ibid., p. 5, 148). Cremo notes that the Hindu time scale is compatible with that of traditional Darwinism (ibid., p. 6).

17 Widely acclaimed Christian author Philip Johnson has made the disclaimer that age is unimportant: "Many people assume that anyone who advocates 'creation' endorses the 'young earth' position and attributes the existence of fossils to Noah's flood. . . . Persons who believe that the earth is billions of years old, and that simple forms of life evolved gradually to become more complex forms including humans, are 'creationists' if they believe that a supernatural Creator not only initiated this process but in some meaningful sense *controls* it in furtherance of a purpose," P.E. Johnson, *Darwin On Trial* (Downers Grove, IL: InterVarsity, 1991), p. 4. Without intending to, Johnson has here made a concise statement of key *Hindu* beliefs about origins, except that in Hinduism, the Creator is not the God of the Bible. Such a statement does *not* fit biblical creation. Unfortunately, Johnson has been preceded by a long line of Christian academic thought which chooses to belittle biblical claims of recent creation. For example, scholar Edward J. Young in his otherwise excellent book, *Thy Word Is Truth* (Grand Rapids, MI: Eerdmans, 1957, p. 169–170), says, "The long ages of geology may indeed have occurred. . . . We incline toward the view that the days [of creation] were periods of time longer than twenty-four hours. We do this . . . upon exegetical grounds." Yet he nowhere says what these "exegetical grounds" might be.

However, Edward J. Young held a high view of Scripture compared to influential scholars such as Bernard Ramm (*The Christian View of Science and Scripture*, Grand Rapids, MI, Eerdmans, 1954) and Russell L. Mixter (*Evolution and Christian Thought Today*, Grand Rapids, MI, Eerdmans, 1959). Ramm and Mixter placed the modern views of "science" (i.e., evolution) before the Bible and no doubt shaped the views of many.

18 This Hindu version of creation has been dubbed "Krishna creationism" in a sympathetic review of *Forbidden Archeology* by K.L. Feder in *Geoarcheology*, vol. 9, p. 337–340; in Cremo, *Forbidden Archeology's Impact*, p. 101.

19 In 1997, a new sitcom went on the air called "Dharma & Greg." Dharma is the Hindu word for "fate." How significant is this first explicitly Hindu-oriented program? Consider that in 1965 the sitcom *Bewitched* introduced a seemingly harmless version of the occult into the Western mainstream. Now the occult permeates our culture via the sale of items such as the Harry Potter children's books, one of the highest selling children's series of all time. The occult mindset is also behind tragedies like the one at Columbine High School in Littleton, Colorado.

Academic journals such as *American Anthropologist* are noting the New Age trend: "New Age titles in bookstores . . . now occupy whole sections of their own — the shamanism, goddess worship, and New Age sections. These shifts reflect social and cultural developments that are well underway not only in this country but all over the world . . ." (cited in Cremo, *Forbidden Archeology's Impact*, p. 52). Cremo himself acknowledges that multiculturalism is part of the agenda to further force Hinduism into the mainstream: "Transnationalism and multiculturalism are not merely concepts entertained by department chairs and university administrators; they are brute objective realities" (p. 27) — i.e., they are part of an agenda which is unfolding.

20 E. von Daniken, *Chariots of the Gods?* (New York, NY: Bantam, 1974), p. 38–40, 56–59.

21 Fuller, *Blavatsky and Her Teachers*, p. 48, 197.

22 *Sky and Telescope* cover, vol. 88, no. 5, May 1992; accompanying article: R.T. Feinberg, "Pulsars, Planets, and Pathos," p. 493–495.

23 R. Naeye, "Two New Solar Systems,"*Astronomy*, vol. 24, no. 4, April 1996, p. 50–55.

24 A.M. MacRobert and J. Rother, "The Planet of 51 Pegasi," *Sky and Telescope*, vol. 91, no. 1, January 1995, p. 38.

25 Naeye, "Two New Solar Systems," p. 50–55.

26 M. Bales et al., "A Planet Orbiting the Neutron Star PSR1329-10," *Nature*, vol. 352, 1991, p. 311–313.

27 MacRobert and Rother, "The Planet of 51 Pegasi," p. 38–40.

28 Ibid.

29 M. Mayor and D. Queloz, "A Jupiter-Mass Companion to a Solar-Type Star," *Nature*, vol. 378, 1995, p. 355–359.

30 R. Cowen, "Two Extra-solar Planets May Hold Water,"*Science News*, vol. 149, no. 4, 1996, p. 52.

31 Ibid.
    M.D. Lemonick, "Searching for Other Worlds," *Time*, vol. 147, no. 6, February 5, 1996, p. 52–57.

32 Cowen, "Two Extra-solar Planets May Hold Water," p. 52.

33 Ibid.

34 R. Jayawardhana, "Wobble Worlds," *Scientific American*, vol. 281, no. 3, September 2000, p. 62. This article also discusses other objects of apparently stellar status which are presented as extrasolar planets.

35 T.P. Snow, *Essentials of the Dynamic Universe* (St. Paul, MN: West Pub. Co., 1987), p. 485.

36 T. Dobzhansky et al., *Evolution* (San Francisco, CA: W.H. Freeman, 1977), p. 366.

37 J.F. Baugher, *On Civilized Stars* (Englewood Cliffs, NY: Prentice-Hall, 1985), p. x–xi.
    D. Overbye, "Is Anyone Out There?" *Discover*, vol. 3, no. 3, March 1982, p. 22.
    Snow, *Essentials of the Dynamic Universe*, p. 499.

38 G.M. Kanon, *The Great UFO Hoax* (Lakeville, MN: Galde Press, 1997), p. 31.

39 J.A. Keel, *Operation Trojan Horse* (Lilburn, GA: IllumiNet Press, 1996), p. 192–222.

40 D. Overbye, "Is Anyone Out There?" p. 22.

41 Ibid., p. 23.